WAYLON

WAYLON

TALES OF MY OUTLAW DAD

TERRY JENNINGS

WITH DAVID THOMAS

NEW YORK   BOSTON

Hachette Books
Hachette Book Group
1290 Avenue of the Americas
New York, NY 10104
HachetteBookGroup.com

Originally published as a hardcover and ebook by Hachette Books.

First trade paperback edition: May 2017

Hachette Books is a division of Hachette Book Group, Inc.
The Hachette Books name and logo is a trademark of Hachette Book
Group, Inc.

The publisher is not responsible for websites (or their content) that are not
owned by the publisher.

The Hachette Speakers Bureau provides a wide range of authors for
speaking events. To find out more, go to www.hachettespeakersbureau.com
or call (866) 376-6591.

LCCN: 2015959619
ISBN: 978-0-316-39010-1

Printed in the United States of America

LSC-C

10 9 8 7 6 5 4 3 2

I dedicate this book first and foremost to my best friend, my Lord and Savior Jesus Christ. His mercy and loving kindness to me is better than life itself.

To my wife, Debra, for her endless love and for fighting the good fight of faith for me long before I ever knew I was in a war.

To our son Joshua, who brightens and energizes life itself, and to my sons Whey and Johnny for your patience and love through some trying times over the years!

And last but not least, to one of the sweetest ladies I know, Aunt Bobbie Nelson, for the big role she played in changing my life and for introducing me to my beautiful wife. I love you dearly.

IN LOVING MEMORY

To my father, Waylon Jennings, and my mother, Maxine Law-
rence Hines; my grandparents William Albert Jennings and
Lorene Beatrice Jennings; my sister Julie Rae Jennings and
her son, Taylor Jennings; my sister Deana Jennings; my cousin
Justin Jennings; Ralph "Mr. Moon" Mooney; Joe B. Mauldin;
Dan "Bee" Spears; Randall "Poodie" Locke; William Hugh
"Billy" Nelson; and the Reverend Will D. Campbell.

CONTENTS

FOREWORD: DIAMONDS AND DIRT, HEARTS AND HURT

Waylon Jennings's renegade image and unique cutting-edge music were mesmerizing. His songs and genius came so gut deep and honest that imitators sounded foolish when they would try to mimic his style. I had always wanted to meet him and he was curious about me—the guy from the Beatles who produced country records. We met in 1973 in the ballroom at Nashville's Sheraton Hotel during the annual Country Music Convention in Nashville, Tennessee. Like everything Waylon, it was like a scene from a Sergio Leone movie. A disheveled cowboy and a Hollywood rocker abruptly coming face-to-face in the middle of a crowded, smoke-filled room. Something clicked between us that night that led to a five-year journey as close friends and a fascinating producer-artist relationship.

There were three people, though, who traveled with him for a much longer ride into the world of cowboy superstardom: one a fledgling child, one a rebellious "rock it to the max" youth, and one a man who grew into adulthood roaring alongside a legend. They are one person—Terry Jennings, his firstborn. Terry saw, felt, and tasted it all from a unique perspective—a child growing into manhood at his dad's side, looking on in amazement at something that was beyond his comprehension. As the years rolled by, he became a roadwise sidekick experiencing the madness and glory of riding hard and far with his ol' man. He inherited the rebellious freedom imparted in him through the dramatic experience of watching his dad's dreams unfold, falter, ignite, flame out, and then skyrocket to heights of dizzying success. There they were, a father and son, a boy and the legend known to us as Hoss, roaring down the never-ending highway to the next gig. We called Waylon "Hoss" because he called us that first.

Hillbilly Central, Tompall Glaser's studio and offices on Nineteenth Avenue South, was where the rough riders of country music gathered during the heart and heat of the early outlaw years. We were outside of Sixteenth and Seventeenth Avenues (Music Row) where the good ol' boys made the noise. I guess you could say we were known as the bad ol' boys that just annoys. We liked it off to the side and thrived on being a pain in the aspirations of the establishment. It was unbridled madness at Hillbilly Central—it rocked and it roared, it stumbled and soared...it was all about lyrics and a chord. It was heartfelt, it was lunacy, it was absurd, it was brazenly beautiful—one thing for sure, it seldom slept. Gathered into its heart and halls was the wildest assemblage of outlaws and outsiders—dudes and drifters, cowboys and cliffhangers, gentlemen and gutter balls, the famous and the forlorn, making music and history with some of Nashville's leading songwriters and pickers of the day. The carpet smelled and the music swelled out of every corner of that building. I know I will never hear music that good again, feel more wild and free, or stay up that many days in a row. As Captain Midnight, one of our most beloved sidekicks, so aptly put it, "Often we stayed up for six nights, and it felt like a week."

There are many stories about Waylon, but if you were around him long enough it soon became apparent he was a story all to himself. He didn't need to tell his story; the story told him—the road man, the guitar man, the songwriter man, the impossible-to-pin-down man, the family man, the creative genius man, the quiet man, the king-of-the-six-day-roar man, the uncommon man, the legendary man, the badass man, the kind man, the singer-of-sad-songs man, and the repeatedly disappearing man...they are all in this book.

Around the edges and often underfoot was a kid watching from a distance, and before long he became an integral part of the story, mimicking us with youthful exuberance. If our cars, cowboy hats, or drugs were ever missing we knew where to find them...just look for Terry. But that was a long time ago, and now, as he graciously shares his touching recollections on these pages, you not only get to see the distant view from an ever-ramblin' tour bus, but in *Waylon: Tales of My Outlaw Dad* you get a closer look from the open window of Terry's heart. This is the most unique insider look at country music's most famous outlaw you will ever read.

For those of us who were there, Nashville, Tennessee, was the home of our diamonds and our dirt, our hearts and our hurt. Some of us came to Music City from places far away— its backbeats and backstreets drawing us like a magnet. Some stayed and in time some drifted away, each one sheltering deep inside the magic of country music's most dynamic and touching artist as part of their forever.

Waylon Jennings laid down his guitar for the last time on February 13, 2002, and headed out to meet his Heavenly Father.

Terry Jennings moved back to the arid lands where it all began, and today he walks the quiet roads of small-town Texas with treasured memories of his father closely wrapped around his heart.

Thank you, Terry, for letting us join you on a ride that will never be forgotten...

God bless us all,
Ken Mansfield
Author, award-winning producer, and former U.S. manager of Apple Records

INTRODUCTION

Waylon Jennings was the greatest Outlaw country musician to grace this earth and arguably the best-ever guitar player in country music.

More important to me, Waylon Jennings was my dad.

I had a complicated relationship with Dad. Our relationship was great, but it was complex. Sometimes we were father-son, sometimes we were boss-employee, and other times we were more like brothers.

He and my mom split when I was five, and we were apart a lot after their divorce. Dad would schedule shows near where we lived in Texas so he could see me and my brother and sister two or three times a year. And then we were around each other all the time when, after the ninth grade, I dropped out of school and traveled with him as part of his road crew.

"Come saddle up with me, son," he told me, "and let's ride."

And ride we did.

During my thirteen years on the road with him, Dad trusted me to look out for him. I became his buffer against the pitfalls of celebrity. He also called on me to bring drugs to him when he was hooking up with some woman in the band's hotel.

Sometimes we were Andy and Opie; sometimes we were Homer and Bart.

But always, my dad and I were best friends. I've always been proud to be known as Waylon Jennings's oldest son. I called him Dad as a kid, but that didn't feel right around the crew. Yet I couldn't call him Waylon, either. So I started calling him the Ol' Man.

He pulled me aside. "What's this, you calling me the Old Man all the time?"

"I'm not calling you the *Old* Man," I explained. "I'm calling you the *Ol'* Man."

"Oh" was all he said, and nothing more came of it until he named his next album *Ol' Waylon*.

You had to be close to my dad to understand how good of a person the Ol' Man was, but *everybody* knew Waylon Jennings was one of the best country musicians ever. I say he was *the* best, but I do acknowledge my bias.

Dad was the first so-called Outlaw artist in Nashville to succeed at bucking the Nashville System that had dominated, and even stifled, country music with its heavy-handed way of choosing which songs an artist recorded and how those songs sounded. My dad was a musical renegade—a rebel, you could say—and became *the* major influence on country music's Outlaw movement by refusing to conform to the System. He fought to maintain creative control over his albums, and his success brought life back into country music. His songs were about real life, about drinking, drugs, women, hardworking men, and honky-tonk heroes. His music was driven by rock 'n' roll, resisting the trend toward more strings in the background. He didn't want his distinctive sound softened; he wanted it raw.

Dad's boot to the System opened doors for fellow artists like Johnny Cash, Willie Nelson, Kris Kristofferson, Hank Williams Jr., and Billy Joe Shaver, Nashville veterans whose careers were revived by the movement. Dad and Willie, in particular, drew on the energy being generated in their home state of Texas, where Willie chose to live and play to fight the system from the outside. Buoyed by their increasing popularity in Texas, Dad and Willie would meet in Austin to plan their attack on Nashville producers and record labels.

I realized my dad was big-time long before those battles, in 1964, when I was in the second grade. Up until then, I hadn't really considered the fact that my dad was a musician to be particularly special, even though some of my friends tried to convince me otherwise. Their dads were plumbers, bankers, and salesmen, and my dad played guitar and sang. To me, there was nothing different about any of them.

In hindsight I probably should have realized it on the day a few years earlier when he called all of us into the living room, saying he wanted to show us something. Mom and Julie took a seat on the couch with Dad, and I sat on the floor. Dad told me to turn on the TV. I got up because, as a high-energy three-year-old, I was basically the family's remote control back then. The television warmed up, and as the picture emerged from within that dark screen, there was Dad on the TV, singing a song. I was excited and confused. How could Dad be sitting there on the couch and at the same time be singing on TV?

I kept asking how that was possible. Mom and Dad gave up on convincing me to settle down and watch and listen, so they just laughed at my bewilderment. Julie, who was eighteen months younger than me, didn't say anything—she just took turns staring at the TV and then Dad.

But the incident still didn't change my image of Dad. If he had been on TV regularly, that would have been something special. I watched a lot of TV, and I thought actors were really, really cool. But my dad, he was Dad. I didn't look at him as being anything else, especially famous.

The first indication that I might be missing something regarding my dad's status came that day in second grade. We had been separated by divorce for a few years, with us kids living with Mom in Texas. When she got pregnant by a married man she had been seeing, my brother, my sister, and I moved out to Phoenix, Arizona, for a while to live with Dad, his second wife, and their adopted daughter.

On my first day in my new school, the teacher introduced me to the class and asked me what my dad did for a living.

"He's a singing star," I answered.

My new classmates laughed.

"No," the teacher interrupted. "He's not kidding." Then she pulled out one of Dad's records. She was a fan.

The other kids stopped laughing.

That was when I began to think that perhaps my dad was a little cooler than most.

I was a teenager when I saw firsthand just how big a deal my dad truly was. Traveling with him as one of his crew members, I really got to witness how people would go gaga over him. Particularly women.

I loved my dad, and even though he was absent for big pieces of my young childhood, I never possessed any ill will toward him. Joining him on the road brought us closer together, and we made up for missed time for the next thirty years until he passed away.

Dad, boss, best friend. He was all those to me, and now, fourteen years after his passing, I still revel every day in the fact that I am Waylon Jennings's oldest son. I had a backstage pass to the life of "the Best Outlaw Ever!" and I can tell you that he wasn't what he was often made out to be.

Dad was a trusting soul, but he possessed a bad habit of trusting people he shouldn't have, and as a result, he made just about every mistake possible during his career.

I'll admit he could be an ornery cuss at times. He received criticism for his quick exits after shows. But he had to scoot. Fans would get fanatical over my dad, and he hired people—members of the Hells Angels, no less—to make sure the more determined ones couldn't get to him.

He didn't like granting interviews to the press and DJs, either. Too many times he had woken up to an article in the morning paper that said the exact opposite of what he had told the reporter. As for country music DJs, back then they tended to drink a lot. Few people knew how much Dad disliked being around alcohol and drunks, even if they were the DJs who determined which albums hit the airwaves.

Somehow, somewhere along the way, the label *outlaw*

unfortunately became associated with him more as a person than as a musician. It's true that Dad was not always the loyal husband he has been portrayed to be. When he was married, he had girlfriends. When he divorced, he had another woman—or two or three—whom my sister, my brother, and I referred to as his "wife in waiting." That was another reason he darted for the doors after a show—he had people waiting on him. And by people, I mean women. Dad kept three or four hotel rooms on the road in the early '70s. One was for him and my stepmom, Jessi Colter, and the other two or three were for his girlfriends.

The womanizing slowed in the mideighties, after Dad got off drugs and became more of a family man. Those of us on the crew began noticing that, for some reason, the ladies in the audience stopped yanking off their tops and throwing their bras and panties at him on the stage. When Dad did receive an in-show message from one adoring fan with a strong throwing arm surpassed only by her lack of subtlety, he told me, "Guess what—a woman threw her panties onstage." It was Dad's way of saying, *Look, son, the Ol' Man's still got it.*

That was the kind of relationship we had. I mean, what kind of a dad would brag to his son about having a pair of panties thrown at him? I suppose the same kind who would sit around and do drugs with his son, or dispatch his son on a pot run because the girl in the hotel room he was visiting wanted some.

Unconventional? Sure. But we definitely were close.

Dad wrote his memoir in 1996. Almost two decades later, as I tell what life was like with my dad, I am amazed at where he stands now in the country music industry. He never thought—and neither did I, for that matter—that once he died, his music would remain relevant like it has. For that I have to thank the old singers, like Willie Nelson, and some of the newer singers, like Jamey Johnson, because it seemed like every year, especially after Dad died, his name would come up at the Country Music Association awards.

Dad would have found that funny, considering that he never really got along with the CMA. As he used to say, "Nashville is hard on the living, but they speak well of the dead." That has been the case with Dad.

He left his mark in the way that he changed country music. Look at the Outlaw musicians today. They are trying to achieve the stature my dad did. They're all trying to become what he was, and I don't blame them.

Waylon Jennings was an incredible singer, songwriter, and guitar player. My dad was a wonderful man to be around. He could be childish and he could be intelligent. He was easy to make mad and easy to make happy. My dad was a complicated man.

But all in all, he was a great ol' man.

WAYLON

1

W-A-Y-L-O-N

Folks in West Texas, where my dad grew up, like to claim they live in God's country. Perhaps so, but it's also the devil's playground when he gets to whipping up sandstorms.

God blessed my dad with a soaring baritone voice and guitar skills so distinctive that true country music fans need only a handful of notes to recognize that their ears are being gratified by a Waylon Jennings tune. And to think that one of the greatest musicians to ever grace God's green earth once was sure he would become a preacher.

Not just any preacher, mind you, but a Church of Christ preacher.

In those days, the Church of Christ believed that musical instruments in church were as sinful as doing drugs and chasing women. So had Dad gone down that path, he would have been forbidden from ever taking a guitar onto a platform. Oh, well. In the end, Dad didn't do well with the drug and women prohibitions, either.

Dad was a smart man, always on the ready to dispense sage

advice—and his ability to quote Scripture would shock many—
but despite my dearth of divine insight, I think Dad chose the
correct path after all. Even to this day, I have to chuckle when
I think about my dad the "outlaw," whose rebellious nature
paved the path for a whole new subgenre of country music,
trying to convince people to follow the straight and narrow.

Littlefield, Texas, with a population on the south side of four
thousand, was Dad's hometown. His abilities with a guitar and
Buddy Holly got Dad out of West Texas, but nobody ever got
West Texas out of Dad. Littlefield was a straight shot northwest
up U.S. Highway 84 out of Lubbock, although in that wide-open
portion of the Lone Star State, most trips were a straight shot.
The drive would take about forty-five minutes unless the devil
was whipping up trouble, in which case you'd have to stop when
the dust got so thick you could barely see past the hood of your
car. I swear, the way the wind blew anything loose from the
west, the New Mexico–Texas border should have kept creeping
eastward, because anything in New Mexico that wasn't heavy
or tied down wound up deposited on the South Plains.

Dad loved West Texas. The people were as true as two plus
two equals four, and the music there was country. Good country. *Pure* country. Heck, the music was so good there that
West Texas boasts its own official music hall of fame. My dad,
Buddy Holly, Mac Davis, Sonny Curtis, Joe Ely, and a whole
playlist full of others all hailed from West Texas.

Yes, West Texas was home to great musicians, and Dad
always considered it his home, even when he lived in Nashville. It was through those West Texas roots that Dad drew
the values and experiences that influenced a lifetime of lyrics.

Rich in Spirit

I believe all the "begat" passages in the Bible are there for a purpose, and I believe where a person comes from is just as important as where they're going. In fact, the former determines the latter.

Dad was born June 15, 1937, in a farmhouse right outside of Littlefield. The first-time parents were William Albert and Lorene Beatrice Jennings. Grandpa, like his parents and five younger siblings, worked as a laborer on cotton farms, pounding the ornery soil with a hoe from sunup to sundown as long as the weather permitted. And it had to be real ugly for the weather to not be permissible. His family would also work odd jobs for extra money. Finding the jobs was more of a concern than finding the time to work them, despite their long days in the fields. If they could find an extra job, they would find the time.

Living in tents and lean-tos, they needed every penny they could pick up. You've heard of dirt-poor? The Jennings clan was so poor that they lived and slept on dirt floors. But because they were surrounded by family and faith, they never considered themselves impoverished. They were raised understanding that money was not the measure of a man. In what mattered most—faith and family—they considered themselves wealthy.

Every Sunday morning, Sunday evening, and Wednesday night, they attended the local Church of Christ. Their work schedules, as time-consuming as they were, always revolved around attending church. If they went to church, God would provide them with chances to work.

Most Saturday nights farm owners took turns hosting dances, opportunities for families in the community not only to come together, eat, visit, and have a good time, but also to separate themselves from their back-breaking jobs that never seemed to allow a person to get ahead financially. Most farmhands' greatest hope was not of a better job, but of being able to keep the job with which the good Lord had blessed them. Grandpa, a self-taught musician, earned a little extra money at many of the dances by singing and playing his guitar and French harp.

Grandma was the oldest of seven children. Somehow, she spiritually survived being the product of a Baptist father and a Jehovah's Witness mother. That made for some real interesting family discussions about religion that had a way of becoming heated. Naturally, when she married Grandpa, she added to her religious diversity by joining him in the Church of Christ. Grandma grew up working on the farm owned by her father, Blevins Shipley. My great-grandpa would say that during the Great Depression, a family could afford to have only one milk cow, so instead of killing his extras, he gave one cow to each family farm that did not already have one.

I grew up hearing bleak stories about life during the Depression—how farmers couldn't afford to hire workers—even considering the low labor cost—so they just bred and raised their own. Parents were in control of their kids back then and knew that the key to keeping them out of serious trouble was to put them to work. Idle hands were the devil's workshop, so they made sure their kids' hands didn't become idle.

After my grandparents married, my grandmother's father was none too thrilled going to bed in his home at night with visions of his daughter sleeping on a dirt floor. When Grandma became pregnant a few months after the wedding, he helped Grandma and Grandpa purchase a new home on Austin Avenue.

With a small house in town, Grandma and Grandpa were on their way to living the American dream, and they worked every odd job they could find to keep the dream alive. No work was too hard or dirty, and no pay was too small to turn down. As long as the work was honest, they were always willing to do it. "Ten dollars a week," Grandpa used to preach to us, "is better than no dollars a week."

Because doctors couldn't peek inside the package like they do now and tell expectant parents the baby's sex ahead of time, my grandparents had no idea whether their firstborn would be a boy or a girl. But Grandpa did know that if it was a boy, his initials would have to be *W.A.* His dad, Grandpa Gus, gave his first son the initials *W.A.* to honor his father, and he'd stated his desire that each subsequent firstborn Jennings son be a *W.A.*

When Dad arrived, he was given the strong name of Wayland Arnold. My grandma had liked the name Gayland, for some reason, and she changed the "G" to a "W" to come up with Wayland.

One of the first well-wishers was a professor and preacher from nearby Wayland Baptist College who had been dispatched to Littlefield to thank the family for naming their son after the school. To Grandma and Grandpa, only one kind of church taught the true Gospel, and if you weren't from a Church of Christ you were not able to fully understand, much less preach or teach, the Word of God.

"I'm sorry, but you must be mistaken," Grandma told the

visitor. "I did not name my child after your school. I named my son Waylon—W-A-Y-L-O-N—Arnold Jennings. If the name showed up on the birth certificate to say any different, they clearly misunderstood what I said."

But "Wayland" had been written onto the birth certificate, and that remained my dad's legal name.

Zipping Through Life

Dad must have had a guardian angel watching over him. After a full-term pregnancy and smooth delivery in a farmhouse, Dad came out healthy. But soon there were signs that something was wrong. Dad wouldn't take breast milk. Grandma tried cow's milk as a substitute, but Dad wouldn't take that, either. He grew sickly, but after several hospital visits, the doctor was still puzzled.

After the doctor told Grandma he had run out of ideas on what could be causing Dad's sickness, she was standing outside the hospital holding Dad and crying when an older lady approached to ask if she needed help. Grandma explained the problem and how she feared for her son's life. The woman suggested Grandma try feeding Dad warm goat's milk. Grandma followed the recommendation, and Dad couldn't drink enough. Grandma forevermore claimed the woman represented a divine intervention that saved Dad's life.

When Dad was two, Grandma delivered him a partner in crime—a brother named Thomas Lee. The only things Dad and Tommy didn't get into as boys were the things they didn't think of.

One day when Dad was five, he was walking atop a wood rail fence and fell. He landed on a sand fighter, a piece of farm equipment with long, sharp, metal spikes that farmers would drag across the land to turn the dirt enough to keep those West Texas winds from blowing it all away. One of those spikes lodged into the bone in Dad's left leg, just above his ankle. The injury caused growth in that leg to be stunted.

Dad always appeared to be leaning to his left, and later in life he would buy two pairs of shoes, with each pair a different size so he could have one pair that fit properly. But back then, it was difficult enough for my grandparents to afford keeping their kids in one pair of shoes each, so Dad walked around most of his younger years with one shoe either too loose or too tight.

When people ask how tall my dad was, I answer, "Six foot one or six foot two, depending on which leg he's standing on." Dad's left-leaning stance gave him a look and style all his own on stage. Later artists copied Dad's stance not knowing the sand fighter left him no choice but to stand that way. That left leg and foot also were the sources of severe health problems later in Dad's life.

Dad and Uncle Tommy did not lack courage. Common sense sometimes, but never courage. One of my favorite stories of Dad's from his growing-up days involved a self-made zip line. Dad and Uncle Tommy observed some other boys having a ball with a zip line they had constructed in a vacant lot by tying one end of a long rope to a branch up in a tree, pulling the rope tight, and tying it to a stake they drove into the ground. Dad and Tommy looked on as the boys took turns placing a leather strap over the rope, grabbing a tight hold of both ends of the strap, and gliding to the ground. They wanted to join in, but they weren't friends with the boys, and the boys didn't seem interested in entertaining guests. Dad and Tommy also were outnumbered, so they couldn't bully their way into the fun.

That left my dad and uncle no choice but to build their own zip line. Being a part of the Jennings line, they naturally felt compelled to outdo their zip-line competitors. They found another vacant lot with an old oak tree, but they couldn't improve on the boys' tree. They would just have to go higher in their tree. Instead of rope, they attached an old steel cable. The cable was stronger than rope and could be stretched tighter with no slack, so that would allow them to descend faster. The steel cable would have cut through leather in no time at all, so the two came up with a stroke of genius: thread the cable through a short piece of old iron pipe as a handle before staking the cable to the ground. All that was left was to hustle up some rope to pull the pipe to the top of the cable. Once the rope was in place, they were ready to impress.

Uncle Tommy received the honor of taking the first ride. He climbed high in the tree, carrying the loose end of the rope. At the top of the zip line, he pulled the hand grip into position with the aid of the pull rope, untied the rope, and secured a firm grip on the pipe. Then Uncle Tommy set sail.

The new zip line worked great for about three feet. Something about the combination of the steel cable, the iron pipe, my uncle's weight, and the unaccounted-for factor of friction caused the handle to come to a complete stop. The pipe wouldn't slide any farther down the cable, and Tommy couldn't work the pipe back up the cable toward the tree.

Uncle Tommy took the lone option that remained and let go of the pipe. He landed in the hospital for X-rays. The cast and sling on Tommy's broken arm made it that much more difficult for him and Dad to convince the other boys in town that their project had not failed, despite the fact, as everyone should have known, "Jenningses don't fail."

We may fall, but we don't fail.

God, Family, and Music

Grandma and Grandpa's family found the most joy from two sources.

First, and undisputedly so, was their love of God. Grandma and Grandpa believed their most important purpose as parents was to make sure all their children had a true understanding of the Word of God. Reaching that goal required attending church three times a week, no exceptions. So pronounced was their devotion that through Dad's midteens, he dreamed and talked often of one day becoming an ordained minister for the Churches of Christ. Dad studied his Bible with determination, and his knowledge of Scripture would have run laps around some preachers I've heard.

Second, the family loved music. In the 1930s and '40s, people could go to the picture show if they had the money for a ticket, or they could listen to the radio if they could afford one and possessed the needed power source. For the Jenningses, music became a cherished and cost-free form of family fun and entertainment.

That always confused me a little, what with the Church of Christ prohibiting musical instruments. The congregation sang from hymnals, but the addition of a single note from a single instrument to any song would have secured for the offender a one-way ticket straight to hell. Outside of church, though, musical instruments were a staple in the Jennings family, especially guitars and a piano. Grandpa showed Dad and Uncle Tommy how to play three notes on the guitar, and the boys thought they were Gene Autry, Ernest Tubbs, and, as their skills progressed, Hank Williams.

Uncle Tommy loved to sing and play, but by age seven or eight, my dad was obsessed with the guitar. From the first time his fingertips trekked across the strings on Grandpa's old guitar, all Dad wanted to do was sing, play, and create his own music. When he wasn't near a guitar, he would pick up a stick or anything similar he could get his hands on and pretend he was playing on a stage in some place other than West Texas.

As Dad was closing in on his ninth birthday, James joined the family as the third Jennings son. Growing up, James D., as he was called, wanted to be with his older brothers all the time, but Dad and Uncle Tommy didn't want James D. slowing their adventures. They would often send little James D. on errands for items that most times didn't exist.

Before James D. had a bicycle like his older brothers, Dad and Uncle Tommy would tell him that he could go places with them as long as he kept up. Those two played every mean trick they could think of on James D. That forced James D. to become meaner, tougher, stronger, and faster than Dad and

Tommy. James D. feared no one or no thing. Just ask those who stepped into James D.'s path, and they'll confirm I'm telling the truth. Even today, you still don't want to mess with James D.

In 1954, when Dad was seventeen, the youngest Jennings—Phillip Doyle—arrived. Dad and his girlfriend at the time nicknamed him Bimbo when he was a baby, and they would sing to him, "Bimbo, Bimbo, where you gonna go-e-o. Down the street to see your little girl-e-o." *Bimbo* was soon shortened to *Bo*, and Phillip Doyle has been simply Bo ever since.

Dad's love of music only increased as he grew older. He entered any and all talent contests he could find, and he won at least most of them. His obsession led to him landing a fifteen-minute spot on KVOW radio in Littlefield at age fourteen. Dad was given five minutes for news, five minutes for recorded music by his favorite artists, and five minutes to play and sing his favorite songs. At that point, Dad was in high cotton.

Dad started his first band with friends, Waylon Jennings and the Texas Longhorns, that played country-western swing at local dances and parties. After more than a year of playing nearby shows and festivals, Dad was introduced to a local group called Buddy and Bob.

The Buddy in this duo was Buddy Holly.

2

OUT OF WEST TEXAS

The local newspaper's wedding announcement for my mom and dad left out one detail: which member of the wedding party was holding the shotgun.

Dad had been dating Maxine Carroll Lawrence, a beautiful young lady from a nearby high school he had met at a beauty contest she won, and they had developed a close relationship. On at least one occasion, ignoring a few key passages from the Good Book my dad had intended to preach from, they got a little too close.

When Mom informed my dad that she was pregnant, there was only one honorable thing to do. New Mexico did not require a blood test before a couple married, and on Christmas Eve, 1955, they drove sixty miles to Clovis, New Mexico, where the eighteen-year-olds who had been caught with their hands in each other's cookie jars—figuratively speaking, of course—made their "for better or for worse" promises in the home of a Church of Christ preacher. The wedding announcement named their mothers and Uncle Tommy as the sole family members in attendance. Tommy was best man, and the preacher's wife volunteered to serve as maid of honor. I'm guessing the preacher's wife wasn't holding the shotgun.

Subsequent events proved the wedding unnecessary when evidence emerged that my mom wasn't pregnant after all. Despite her late-arriving period, life changes were already well under way. The newlyweds moved into my paternal grandparents' house. Raised that men should always do right by their wives, Dad felt the need to support his new bride. He had already dropped school. While in school Dad had been a right good kicker on his high school team, despite an embarrassing debut in which his first attempt at a kickoff was a big swing and a miss that left Dad flat on his back and the football still on the tee, undisturbed. Now married, he took on additional jobs to support his wife.

Mom stayed in school to finish her senior year. Dad, who kept his small-paying job at KVOW, found extra work when he could, selling clothes in a local department store, driving a school bus, doing a little mechanical work, or working for his dad at whatever the business venture of the moment might be.

Those jobs he performed out of duty. Playing guitar and singing remained Dad's passion. He continued to pick up small gigs around the area and enter as many talent contests as he could. The prizes for winning were small, though, and family members and town folk didn't hesitate to wonder aloud when Waylon was going to realize that playing and singing was a waste of time and then get off his lazy backside and find a real job.

Dad made things worse when his school bus got a flat tire and he refused to change the tire, even if it would cost him his job. He wasn't being lazy, though; he was just afraid to do any job that might hurt his hands. He needed those hands to play his guitar, and he wasn't going to do anything to put his passion at risk.

I don't want to say I wish Dad had felt the same about Mom as he did his music. I think Dad loved Mom very much, and I think she loved him right back. It was just that if they hadn't had to rush into their wedding, they probably would have discovered before they married that they weren't the best of matches.

They were both strong-willed and had quick wits, and yet they were polar opposites. Mom liked to drink; Dad didn't. Dad liked to look nice when he went into town; Mom could not have cared less how she dressed.

They say that opposites attract, but I don't think polar opposites do.

The two interests they most shared were sex and partying. Even their ideas on how best to party were different. Dad liked to party by playing music and hanging out with his music friends. Mom came from a family of bootleggers, and that was reflected in her preference to show off her singing husband while drinking with her parents and their drinking buddies.

It doesn't require a seminary degree to see how Mom's partying ways rubbed Dad's Church of Christ family the wrong way.

Their shared interest in sex brought me into the world on

January 21, 1957. I was the first grandchild on the Jennings side. Not that there had been a long wait, though, because Dad's youngest brother, Bo, arrived just a couple years ahead of me.

What's in a Name?

My parents named me Terry Vance. Terry came from a crooner of the time, Terry Lawrence. Vance came from Vance Reno, the character in the movie *Love Me Tender*, whose brother was played by Elvis Presley.

T.V. proved to be appropriate initials, considering how much television I grew up watching, but my name violated the family tradition of firstborn Jennings boys carrying the initials *W.A.*

Oh, boy, did my name sure set off a firestorm.

"Where's the *W*? Where's the *A*?" Grandpa Jennings demanded. "This can't happen. His name has got to be changed. The oldest of the oldest? This won't do. The firstborn has to be *W.A.*, and it will continue to be that way in this family."

Momma wouldn't budge an inch, and T.V. I remained.

Grandpa never let it go. He died in 1968, when I was eleven, and for the remainder of his life he had continued to pester Dad about my name. I remember once, not long before Grandpa passed away, when I was washing dishes at my aunt's café in Littlefield and my dad called to ask how I would feel about changing my name to Waylon Arnold. He didn't say it was to get his dad off his back, but I knew why he was asking.

"That'd be fine with me if that's what y'all want to do," I told Dad. "But I'm sure everybody will keep calling me Terry."

That nixed for good the idea of changing my name.

Me not being a *W.A.* never was a big deal to me or my dad. Or to anyone other than Grandpa Jennings, for that matter. When my first son was born, though, we made him a *W.A.* by naming him Whey Arron. If I hadn't, Grandpa might have come back out of the grave to give me a piece of his mind.

Grandma Lorene wasn't bothered by my initials. Her main concern was that I would be a healthy baby and be kept safe from the fussing over my name. But she did have a problem with Mom taking me over to her parents' house when my dad would be working or running with his buddies. Grandma thought my mom's family drank too much. "That little baby's going to get hurt over there," she would say.

My mom got pregnant again late in 1957. About that time, Dad got fired from the radio station where he had been working as a full-time DJ. Late at night, he would play Little Richard records. The station owner didn't like that "black devil music" being played on his airwaves and drove up to the station one night and told Dad, "If you ever play that again, I'll fire you." The owner left and started home. Dad promptly placed Little Richard back on the turntable. The owner turned his car around, drove back to the station, and fired Dad on the spot.

The firing turned out to be a stroke of luck. KLVT in Levelland, a bigger sister station twenty-three miles to the south, offered Dad a full-time DJ job. They didn't have to ask Dad twice if he wanted the job, and the three of us moved to Levelland. That was where my sister, Julie Rae, was born the following summer. Her first name came from singer/actress Julie London.

KLVT was the first station I remember visiting with my dad. I was about three at the time. I remember feeling surprised to discover how small the control booth was where he worked. It was downright claustrophobic in there. Dad and I were crammed shoulder to shoulder, a wall of complex electronics and buttons right in front of us. There were so many buttons and switches involved in radio back then that DJs were required to have an electrician's license.

Dad introduced me on the air as his son, and I said a few words. I didn't want to do it again, because I didn't like hearing my own voice come back at me through the speaker.

At the bigger station in Levelland, Dad's fan base grew, and he caught the attention of the Corbin brothers, Sky and Slim. The Corbins had just bought radio station KLLL in Lubbock, the largest city in the South Plains with a population then of about one hundred twenty-five thousand. Dad's witty personality on the air connected with listeners, and Sky and Slim offered Dad a job at their new station, which sat atop the tallest building in Lubbock, the Great Plains Life Building. At twenty-one stories, the building towered over downtown Lubbock and on clear days offered a clear view all the way into next week.

We moved back to Littlefield, and Dad would wake up early in the mornings to make the thirty-five-mile drive to Lubbock and start his show at 5 or 6 A.M. Dad had a problem with oversleeping, however, and wound up moving to an afternoon slot.

I don't remember listening to Dad on the radio much then

because of how early his show was. The music we heard from Dad then came from around the house. We didn't have much money because although Dad was making higher wages at K-Triple-L than he had elsewhere, he still wasn't making much. We would have cheap sunglasses around the house, like the ones you might win as a carnival prize. If Dad felt like playing his guitar, he'd ask if we had any of those sunglasses. If we did, we'd retrieve a pair for him and he'd pop the lens out, carve it into a guitar pick, and play for hours.

Buddy Holly visited the station and its recording studio a lot. Dad had met Buddy back at a talent show at KDAV. Local singers would show up in a parking lot and play and sing, and the station's DJs would select singers to come back for the on-air *Sunday Party*. Buddy was always getting chosen from among the contestants, and Dad got picked a few times, too. A musical community arose out of those days, and they all supported each other. They all wanted to see each other make it, and Buddy was the first one of the bunch to do so.

So Buddy would stop by K-Triple-L when he was in town and hang out. Sonny Curtis, too. Dad liked playing Buddy's records, and Buddy appreciated the support.

Mom liked Buddy, but she didn't like the fact that Buddy would drive up to our house and honk his horn, and then Dad would take off with Buddy to do whatever it was they did together.

With Buddy, Sonny, and all the other cool musicians stopping by KLLL to do interviews, on-air promotions, and jingles, the radio station grew big. Dad's ratings soared, too, as he became one of the hottest personalities in West Texas.

West Texas Meets New York City

Buddy was the biggest thing on radio at the time, and he was flying back and forth to New York City, because he had met his wife there and he also believed New York to be the center of music. Nashville was there for someone wanting good country music, but Buddy had been down that route and Nashville, he felt, wanted to change him. Buddy's grand plan was to create his own record label, and Dad was the first artist he intended to sign.

Late in '58, Buddy was set to record at Norman Petty's studio in Clovis. Buddy stopped off in Littlefield to pick up Dad and take him along. King Curtis was the hottest saxophone player at the time, and Buddy arranged for him to fly in, too.

After Holly's band, the Crickets, had finished their recordings, Buddy had Dad cut two songs, "Jole Blon" and "When Sin Stops," with Buddy producing. "Jole Blon," a Cajun waltz, was pretty funny stuff. Here you had a kid from West Texas singing French lyrics that he could hardly remember, much less understand. Dad and his brothers, and all his family really, got big laughs out of that.

Dad was working his way up, but he still had doubters in town, even among his own family. To them, Dad was chasing a pipe dream, and he needed to give it up and find a reliable job so he could better support Mom and us.

Meanwhile, Buddy was going through a transition period. Buddy's manager, Norman, recognized he was on the verge of losing the goose that laid the golden egg, and in order to keep control over Buddy, held back royalty payments. Buddy needed that money. He also was in the middle of a falling-out with the other two members of the Crickets, because they were West Texas boys through and through, and they didn't want to move to New York City.

The Crickets were a group. But more and more, references were gradually being made to "Buddy Holly and the Crickets," because Buddy was the big draw of the three. Joe B. Mauldin, the bass player, was as humble a guy as there was on earth. I've heard that J. I. Allison, the drummer, and Dad didn't get along. But that couldn't have been further from the truth. Joe B. and J.I. were happy where they were, and Buddy wanted to go out on his own.

Buddy had turned down offers to headline the Winter Dance Party Tour, a series of live shows across the country featuring a variety of musicians. But needing money fast, what with bills coming due and having a wife to support in the big city, Buddy changed his mind and accepted. Buddy needed a band, and he asked guitarist Tommy Allsup to help him put one together. Tommy started working his network.

In early January, when Dad was twenty-one, Buddy stopped by KLLL and asked my dad to play bass for him. Actually, he didn't really ask. He handed my dad a bass and said, "Take this. You have two weeks to practice and meet me in New York City."

"I'm a guitar player," Dad responded. "I don't know how to play bass."

"Two weeks, Waylon. Two weeks," Buddy answered. "You'll figure it out. See ya in New York." Buddy turned and walked out, not allowing Dad another opportunity to balk.

Dad immediately got his hand on everything the Crickets had recorded and started practicing. Dad told me that during those two weeks, he figured out that the bass guitar wasn't anything but the top four strings of a guitar.

Buddy sent Dad a train ticket and a little food money, and Dad left us and the South Plains of West Texas for the concrete jungle of New York City to spend a week at the apartment of Buddy and his wife, Maria Elena, and prepare for the tour.

They say you can tell who the tourists are in New York City because tourists are the ones who are looking up. That was Dad. Buddy hailed a cab while Dad kept gawking at the enormity of the city. A cab pulled to a stop next to them, and a woman ran up to the door and started to get into the backseat. Buddy grabbed her by the arm and said, "Hey, lady, that's *my* cab."

Dad gave Buddy a bad look and followed him into the cab.

"Buddy, that's no way to treat a woman," Dad scolded him. "I know you was raised better than that."

"Waylon," Buddy said, laughing, "you got a lot to learn about life in the big city."

Buddy took Dad to Buddy's agent's office. Dad sat in the reception area while Buddy went in to speak with his agent. Even though they weren't on the top floor of the office building, Dad was sitting in an office much higher than the top floor of the Great Plains Life Building back in Lubbock. It was right then and there that Dad realized just how important his old friend from West Texas had become.

As Dad sat there, nervously minding his own business, people started coming into the office. All were asking for Buddy.

"Is Buddy here?"

"Where's Buddy?"

"I need to talk to Buddy!"

Dad was amazed listening to all the excitement surrounding Buddy's presence.

There are famous photos of Dad and Buddy taken at Grand Central Station. According to Dad, Buddy took him into one of those photo booths where you could get four pictures for a quarter. They came out with pictures of Dad and Buddy, with a smiling Dad in sunglasses and holding a cigarette and Buddy in those unforgettable horn-rimmed glasses and a cigarette dangling from his lips. Those pictures have been in print around the world.

I've read and heard in different places that they took those photos right before they left Grand Central Station for the Winter Dance Party Tour, but I remember Dad telling me they took them when he arrived in New York and Buddy picked him up.

I don't know which it was, and it does make for a better story to believe the photos were from when they were leaving New York. Whichever it was, though, those photos are the last images most of us have of Dad and Buddy together.

3

AFTER THE MUSIC DIED

I was still only two years old when Buddy Holly died in a plane crash. I didn't know anything about Buddy.

We had a chest of drawers in our living room, and on top was a picture of a friend of Dad's wearing these funny-looking black glasses. One day that photo disappeared, and we never talked about why. Even as I grew older, Dad never talked about Buddy, and the experience would remain a mystery to me for many years.

Dad's guitar playing abruptly stopped when he came home from the Winter Dance Party Tour, and he began working odd jobs again. Uncle Tommy had a small garage where he worked on cars. Dad worked there for a while, but he didn't like getting his knuckles busted up, so that job didn't last long.

Dad still liked to get down on the floor and play with Julie and me, but it seemed like he was gone from our house most of the time. Even when he was with us, he didn't seem like he was completely there mentally. Dad had always been happy and hyper, but after the picture of his friend disappeared, he became down and jittery. Julie and I spent more time at Grandma and Grandpa Jennings's house than at our own home.

Momma got pregnant late that spring. When that happened, Dad took back his old job at KLLL. We still lived in Littlefield, and the commute was hard on Dad. He occupied the early-morning slot, and there were numerous mornings that Dad's show opened with the dreaded dead air. Dad decided we should move to Lubbock to be closer to the station.

Every so often, the four of us would load up in the car and take Mom to the hospital. The visits were just for checkups, but Julie and I didn't know that. We'd sit in the back of the car while Mom and Dad went inside, and when they'd come back to the car, Julie and I would practically climb over the seat looking for a baby. Each time, we'd slump back into our seats upon learning that we didn't have a new little brother or sister yet.

Finally, on March 21, 1960, our little brother decided to make his grand entrance. Dad chose his first name of Buddy. Mom chose Dean to be his middle name, after Dean Martin.

It wasn't until the fifth grade that I knew who Buddy Holly was, or that he was who my brother was named for. We were back to living in Littlefield then, and my grandparents explained everything about Dad and Buddy Holly to me. Dad never talked to us about Buddy Holly, and none of us ever asked. When I was a teenager and started going on the road with him, the first thing I was told by a crew member was "Don't talk about Buddy."

Later, I saw how sore of a subject it was for him. Whenever someone would bring up Buddy to Dad, he'd get pissed and say, "It's none of your business. Don't ever bring it up again."

The only person I knew of who could get away with making any kind of reference to Buddy was Dan Spears, a bass player. Everyone called him Bee. He worked with Dad on his *Honky Tonk Heroes* album, one of the most important albums in the Outlaw movement, and he worked with Willie Nelson for more than forty years.

Bee knew that Dad was afraid of flying because of what happened to Buddy, at least until Dad got into his cocaine phase and he felt bulletproof, even in an airplane. Before then, though, when we did have to fly, Bee would say when we touched down, "Waylon, you can breathe now. We're on the ground."

Only Bee could get away with saying anything like that. Anyone else, and Dad would have made his distinctive noise that can best be described as a grunt-growl. Anyone who spent time around Dad knew that was his way of saying, *Stop right there and move on to a different subject.* Other than Bee, we steered clear of the topic.

I had been curious about Dad and Buddy, but I knew he didn't want to talk about it, so I had never asked. Then, twenty years after Buddy's death, Dad decided to open up to me about it. Dad had a large room in the back of his house that we called the cave. There was a sofa on one side of the room, another sofa on the opposite side, and two chairs with a table. The room also had a big-screen TV. It was one of those Advent projection televisions that projected the images onto an oval silver screen, and you pretty much had to be sitting in front of the TV to watch it. It was nothing like what we can watch today, of course, but, hey, it was a big-screen TV. (That was back in the days when satellite dishes were all the rage—those huge dishes out in the yard that you would have to go crank to put in the right position for the best reception. The satellite company wound up taking the crank away from us because we'd be high and outside trying to move it into place. "I'm taking the crank with me," one of the guys finally told us. "If it messes up, call me and I'll come fix it.")

One day when I was twenty-two, Dad and I were in the cave and, out of nowhere, he started talking about Buddy Holly. Dad wasn't an emotional guy. Rarely did I see him cry. Whenever something happened, he would always try to turn the event into a life lesson.

"I'm going to tell you what went down," he said to me. "Everybody's been wanting to know."

True to his form, his demeanor was matter-of-fact throughout the story.

Dad told me how the travel from stop to stop on the Winter Dance Party Tour was relentless and the bus had been experiencing problems. An open date on February 2 had been filled with a show in Clear Lake, Iowa, and the next night, everyone would have to be in Moorhead, Minnesota, which was more than 350 miles away. Buddy, frustrated and worn out from all the logistical problems, arranged for a chartered flight into Fargo, North Dakota, which was just across the Red River from Moorhead.

Dad was supposed to be on the flight with Buddy and

Ritchie Valens, who got his seat in a coin flip with Tommy Allsup. But the Big Bopper, J. P. Richardson, had been sick, and Dad told J.P. he would ride in on the bus so J.P. could take Dad's seat on the plane.

Dad and Buddy were in the backstage area after the show at the Surf Ballroom in Clear Lake, and Dad grabbed a couple of hot dogs for him and Buddy. Dad recalled that Buddy was sitting in a cane-backed chair, leaning against the wall. "I understand you aren't going with us tonight," Buddy said to Dad, as they began eating their hot dogs.

"No, the Big Bopper's sick," Dad said. "I told him to take my seat."

"No, you're just scared of flying," Buddy shot back.

"I ain't scared of shit, you son of a bitch," Dad retorted.

"I'll tell you this," Buddy said with a smile on his face. "I hope your old bus freezes up."

"Well," Dad told him, "I hope your old plane crashes."

That was their last conversation, and it haunted Dad for years.

When the bus pulled into Moorhead the next morning, the guy in charge of the hotel told the tour manager, "Get Waylon in here now."

Dad walked through the lobby doors and noticed a newspaper stand with the picture of a plane crash on the front page of the newspaper. He saw what looked like Buddy's glasses lying in the snow in the picture.

"Buddy died in a plane crash last night," Dad was told.

He turned around and walked back out to the bus.

As far as he was concerned, the show was over.

As far as the promoters were concerned, however, the show had to go on.

Releasing the Guilt

The concert in Moorhead went on as scheduled, with Dad doing Buddy's part. He did that for two or three more shows until a Buddy impersonator was brought in to finish the tour.

The promoters had promised Dad that if he would do the first show after the plane crash, they would buy him a plane ticket to Lubbock so he could attend Buddy's funeral. They broke that promise, keeping him on the road instead. Dad didn't get to say good-bye to his friend.

When the tour finished in Springfield, Illinois, Dad and the rest of the tour members returned to New York, and Dad didn't get paid for his work. He didn't have enough money to get home on his own, so he had to call his friend Sonny Curtis to drive up from Lubbock and take him back home.

Life was difficult for Dad when he got back to Littlefield. He was twenty-one at the time, and Buddy was twenty-two. They were just a couple of young knuckleheads cutting up with each other like they always did. Dad felt so guilty about his last words to Buddy.

Dad went on to tell me how Hi-Pockets Duncan, a DJ friend of his, had a long talk with him three months after Buddy's death that helped straighten him out.

"Do you think you're God?" Hi-Pockets asked Dad. "Do you think it was you that made that plane crash? Do you really think Buddy would want you to stop chasing the dream Buddy had for you and you had for yourself? You need to stop this little pity party you're having, pick up the guitar, and get back on your horse and ride."

Dad said Hi-Pockets's firm but gentle talk got him going again.

But still, Dad didn't talk about what happened for those twenty years.

I'm not sure what caused him to open up to me, but he said he wanted me to know about it before he and I went back out on the road again. It could have been because we'd had the Crickets traveling with us, and they had given Dad Buddy's motorcycle as a birthday present. That motorcycle had sat in storage for twenty years and the first time Dad went to kick-start it, that machine started right up.

It also could have been that, by then, I had begun serving as Dad's buffer. Dad didn't like talking to DJs, because too many were drunks and walked around with entitled attitudes. There were lots of DJs who wanted to talk to Dad. He and drunks were a combustible combination, though, and that was why he wanted me to step in, saying to DJs that "Waylon's son is almost as good as being with Waylon himself." So I would keep the DJs busy and entertained so that Dad wouldn't have to deal with them. I'm proud of the fact that during all that time, I only got one DJ cross with us.

"I'm sorry I pissed this guy off," I told Dad. "It was the guy from the local AM station."

"AM?" Dad asked. "We're not going to worry about it."

Anyway, Dad probably knew that once we got back out

onto the road with the Crickets, I was going to be bombarded with questions, and I think he wanted me to answer the questions the way they needed to be answered. I didn't have those answers until our talk in the cave. It was fun to know that Dad had my back and that I also was in a position to have his.

It also could have been that Dad was flat-out tired of people bringing Buddy Holly up and had decided it was time to get his story out there.

When our talk about Buddy was over, I thought, *Wow! I understand why you get so pissed off now.* I gained a sense that day of how Dad felt. It all made sense. I felt relief for Dad that he was able to get it off his chest after all those years.

In 1991, when Reba McEntire lost eight members of her band in a plane crash, she called Dad. He told Reba from his experience that there was no reason for her to feel guilty, that it was not her fault that the plane had crashed. Dad was very concerned about Reba.

"She can't blame herself," he told me. "It wasn't her fault. She loved those guys, but she can't carry that kind of guilt."

He paused.

"I know what it can do to you."

4

OVER A POP GUN?

Dad's getting back into the game following Buddy's death didn't make Momma happy. Not only did he start running around with his musician buddies again, but he also added a newfound friend to the mix: speed.

One reason Dad never really got into alcohol is that he didn't want anything that would bring him down. Uppers provided what Dad was looking for, even though we didn't know he was taking them.

Somehow, despite Mom not liking Dad running with his buddies and Dad bouncing off the walls like a pinball, things seemed pretty much back to normal around our house for the first time since the plane crash. Mom stayed home to take care of us kids, and Grandma and Grandpa Jennings were regularly coming by to check on us.

That Christmas of 1960—our only one in Lubbock—stands out as a time when we were one big, happy family.

I was almost four, and Julie and I were trying to figure out this Santa Claus guy. We couldn't determine how he could get the toys inside our house without a chimney. And how could his reindeer land a sleigh when there was no snow? We never received any answers to our questions—at least, answers that were as smart as our questions.

On Christmas Eve, Mom baked a plate of cookies, we set them out with a glass of milk, and Mom shipped the three of us into the back bedroom so Santa could come do his thing, however he did it.

We stayed back there, as quiet as we'd ever been, anxiously awaiting the arrival of Santa and his reindeer. Then it happened—the jingling of the bells on the reindeer! We rushed to the front door, threw it open, and dashed out onto the front porch to catch Saint Nick by surprise. That darned Santa must have been quick, because there was no trace of him or his reindeer anywhere. If we could have gotten some snow in Lubbock, we at least could have had boot prints and hoofprints to make us happy.

As we turned back toward the inside of our house, our disappointment gave way to screams of joy. Next to the door sat a pile of gifts, built and wrapped by Santa's elves themselves. We carried our gifts inside, and just as we started unwrapping them, the door opened again and there stood Dad. I got a train set, Julie got a doll, and Buddy got a toy truck. We did indeed have a merry Christmas.

I don't know if we were ever as happy as a family as we were that day.

My grandpa on my mom's side died five or six months later in Arizona. Our parents went to Grandpa Lawrence's funeral without us, leaving us with Grandma and Grandpa Jennings in Littlefield. Mom and Dad stayed with Mom's uncle Jigger in Coolidge, about an hour southeast of Phoenix.

After the funeral, the family gathered at Jigger's house and reminisced about the good ol' days. As they talked, Dad got to remembering how much he had liked Arizona when he and Mom had taken me out there to meet Grandpa Lawrence. Jigger told Dad that KCKY, a local radio station, was looking for a DJ. Dad decided to meet the station's owner, Earl Perrin, and ask about the opening. Mr. Perrin offered Dad an afternoon slot, and Dad accepted.

With Dad, things could change quickly, and when he and Mom came home, they announced that we were moving west. We packed everything we could into our car and a small trailer and took off for our new home in Coolidge.

I remember life in Coolidge—a small, dumpy town then—being anything but happy for us. When Dad was at home, he was trying to make Mom happy while at the same time Mom was trying to make Dad unhappy.

I think Momma wanted a husband who went to work in the morning and came home to his family at night. I think Dad wanted a stand-by-your-man kind of wife who people would see was proud to be his wife—in a humble sort of way—when they were out in public.

At that time, neither was getting what they wanted.

KCKY was three blocks from our small apartment. Dad would walk to work in the afternoon so Mom could have our car to get done what she needed to do with us. When he came home, he kissed the family, grabbed a bite to eat, and then took his guitar and hitchhiked to Phoenix, where he could play in bars for tips and hang out with his musician friends. He'd get home late and go through the same routine the next day. I don't think the man ever slept.

Mom was very beautiful, a five-foot-two package of pure dynamite. She was so tiny that she was nicknamed Bitty, which my dad shortened to Bit. Mom was an active person more comfortable in a blouse and a pair of slacks than in a frilly dress or a skirt-and-jacket combo. Far from the prim and proper spouse that Dad would have preferred to have on his arm in public, Mom's idea of socializing was to get loud and raise a ruckus.

Social outings devolved into a competition for the center of attention. Oil and water mix better than Mom and Dad did in public.

Mom would do things just to piss off Dad. She had beautiful, long black hair when they married. She cut it short once just because she knew Dad liked it long.

One day, she sent Dad, Buddy, and me out for a few groceries. Dad asked the clerk for two empty bags in addition to the one bag of our purchases. In front of the apartment, Dad had Buddy squat down into one of the empty bags and me into the other. Dad carried our two bags inside and sat us on the kitchen table. When Momma came in to get the groceries out of the bags, Buddy and I jumped out and yelled, "Boo!"

Mom jumped straight back, gathered herself, and then laughed and exclaimed, "You got me! *You got me!*"

Then there were times like the night Mom was waiting for Dad to come home from work. We were supposed to be in bed, but we watched as Mom stood on a chair with a piece of rope tied around her neck and the other end tied around the lightbulb in the center of the ceiling. When Dad walked through the door, Mom jumped off the chair. The lightbulb broke from the weight and pieces of the broken bulb showered down upon her. She laid there next to the chair motionless, as if she were dead. Dad didn't think it was funny.

I was just confused as to what was happening. To a young kid, each event like that was nothing more than its own event; I wasn't old enough to see the big picture and understand the friction that existed in Mom and Dad's relationship.

Their boiling point came one day when Dad was getting ready to go to work.

Caught in the Middle

I had been bugging Mom and Dad for a toy I had seen on TV, and I knew if one of them would get it for me, my life would be better forever and ever, amen. It was a pop gun—a piece of hollow rubber in the shape of a gun with four plastic balls. You placed a ball into the barrel, like a cork into a bottle. Instead of a trigger, the pop gun had a hand grip. When you squeezed that grip, the gun would make a popping noise and a ball would fly out of the barrel. Then it was time to reload, aim, and fire again. At the time, it had to be the greatest invention in the history of all mankind.

Dad had made one of his all-night trips to Phoenix the previous night, and he was in the shower cleaning up for work.

Mom started dressing me and telling me that I would be going to work with Dad and he would buy me the pop gun I had been begging for. I was so excited that I was a moving target as Mom tried to dress me.

Dad came out of the shower, dressed, and headed out the front door for the station. I ran out behind him, trying my best to keep up with those long steps of his. Dad was across the street when he realized I was chasing after him. Dad stopped to wait for me, and Momma was standing on the sidewalk on our side of the street, with a big tree between her and our apartment.

Dad smiled as I reached him.

"What're you doing, son?"

I could barely get the words out of my mouth.

"Momma said I was going to work with you today and you would buy me a pop gun!"

Dad shot Mom a quick glare, and then he looked down at me and smiled again.

"I'm sorry, son. You can't go to work with me today. I'll take you to get a pop gun when I get home."

My head dropped, and I turned and slowly started walking back across the street to Momma. She laughed.

"Daddy's just kidding you," she told me. "Go on to work with your dad, and he'll buy you a pop gun. Tell Daddy that if he doesn't take you to work with him, he doesn't love you. Go with Daddy and get your pop gun."

That restored my hope, and I started walking back toward Dad.

"Bit, quit it!" Dad yelled at my mom. He softened his tone

to tell me, "Not today, son. We'll get that pop gun when I get home."

Again, my head dropped and I started back toward Momma. She was still laughing.

"Go to work with your dad and get your pop gun," she told me. "Tell Daddy he doesn't love you if he doesn't take you to work with him today."

My emotions were riding a yo-yo string.

"Maxine!" Dad yelled as he headed back across the street toward us. Mom turned to run to the apartment, and her face smacked hard into the thick trunk of that tree.

Next thing I remember, Mom and Dad were in the car and headed for the hospital, with blood flowing from the left side of Momma's lower lip. The emergency room doctor stitched her up in a checkerboard pattern. I distinctly remember those stitches. Before she had them removed, I would go into our parents' bedroom in the morning and touch Mom's stitches to wake her up and let her know that my siblings and I were ready for breakfast.

It was impossible not to notice Mom's stitches, and everyone would ask her about them. She and Dad would tell the same story about the pop gun, but their accounts differed on why she needed the stitches. Dad told people that she had run into the tree; Momma claimed that Dad had gotten mad over the pop gun and hit her. It was Mom's word against Dad's, except for the one witness: their four-year-old son. I told the truth every time, that I saw it happen, and Momma had run into the tree. To those who wanted to believe Dad, my story was true. To those who wanted to believe Momma, I was lying. I never understood why people wouldn't believe me. I saw it all, and I was telling the truth. Whenever Mom would tell her version, I'd even tell her she was wrong, but she'd just laugh it off.

The next big event I can remember came a few months later. We all went back to Grandma and Grandpa Jennings's house in Littlefield. Dad and I were on the front porch, and he was telling me that he had to go and that I was now the man of the house and needed to help Momma with Julie and Buddy. I cried and cried and cried. Dad said he would come back to see us as soon as he could and that no matter what happened or whatever people might say, I was his son, he loved me, and he would always love me.

Grandma tried to pull me back into the house as Dad walked away. I fought her the whole time, yelling, "No! Come back, Dad! Daddy! Daddy! Come back!"

Dad got into his car and drove away.

5

HELL AT HOME

When Dad left, we stayed in Texas with mom.

Dad went back to Arizona. I missed my dad, but living with Grandma and Grandpa was fun because of my uncle Bo. Grandma and Grandpa's youngest was only two years older than me, and we were raised like brothers.

Momma began to mention this woman named Lynne in conjunction with my dad. I didn't know anything about Lynne other than Mom didn't like her and cussed when she talked about her. Dad married Lynne as soon as his divorce from Mom finalized. I was five at the time.

Lynne got pregnant, but they had to abort the baby to save Lynne's life. Lynne really wanted to have a baby, so they adopted a baby girl and named her Tomi Lynne.

Sometime between New Year's Day and my seventh birthday in late January, I met Lynne when we kids went out to Arizona with Grandma and Grandpa to see our new baby sister. I took my train set on the trip so I'd have something to play with. I met a kid in the apartment complex where Dad and Lynne lived and traded him my train set for his toy dump truck. Lynne got mad when she found out, because she thought the train set was broken, and she made me go to the kid and take back the trade.

So Lynne didn't make a strong first impression on me.

Momma had a sister named Claudine, whom everyone called Squawky because she squawked when she talked. Aunt Squawky lived in Irving, Texas, a suburb of Dallas, and Mom wanted to be near her. We moved into a home with another woman who had four kids. So in that house, we had two mothers, no fathers, and seven kids. I attended first grade in Irving, then out of nowhere Mom said she thought it best for Julie, Buddy, and me to move to Arizona and live with Dad and Lynne. We didn't know at the time that Mom had become pregnant by a married man who said he would not leave his wife.

Dad and Lynne had bought a house in Phoenix. Dad was playing at three different bars for money and developing a loyal following for him and his band, the Waylors. What proved to be a big break occurred when he was approached by Jimmy Musiel, the part-owner of Magoo's along with Bob Sikora. Magoo's was one of the bars where Dad had been playing, and Mr. Musiel noticed that the bar was full when Dad played and empty when he played elsewhere.

Mr. Musiel told my dad that he wanted to build a club that would have rock music and go-go girls downstairs and country music upstairs. But Mr. Musiel told my dad he would only build that club if Dad and the Waylors would play there.

Mr. Musiel opened JD's in 1964 to full houses.

While my dad's music career started to take off, life was tough at home. Lynne didn't have much need for the three young mavericks from Texas who had moved in. Perhaps Lynne thought we were moving in on Tomi Lynne's territory. I don't know. But whatever her reason, Lynne made living in Phoenix hell for us kids.

She wouldn't allow us to touch anything of the baby's and didn't tell us why. We learned later that the baby was ill and Lynne was afraid we'd get germs on Tomi's toys if we played with them. It would have been nice to know that, because we assumed Lynne made the baby's toys off-limits because we weren't hers.

Momma delivered our new half sister after we moved to Arizona. I say *half sister*, but that's merely a technical term in our family. Dad told Mom to put his name on the birth certificate as the father, because he wanted all the kids to have the same last name. Only a few of us in the family were told that story by the time Deana had turned fifteen. The rest didn't find out until she was eighteen.

There are seven of us children of Waylon, including Deana, and I consider them all full siblings. Tomi Lynne was adopted by Dad and Lynne. She's my sister. When Dad married his fourth wife, Jessi Colter, she had a five-year-old daughter named Jennifer. I have no blood relation to Jennifer, but she's my sister. That's just the way we Jennings kids are—tight, despite the "normal dysfunctionality" we experienced together. That dysfunction might actually be the reason we became so tight.

After Mom had Deana, she wanted all of us back home with her. The trouble was Dad wanted to keep us, too. Mom came out to Arizona and pulled Julie out of school, took her to the bus station, and returned her to Texas. She tried to take me, too, but the school wouldn't release me to her. Buddy was still at home, because he wasn't old enough for school yet.

That created a lot of drama. Dad and Lynne had me get on the phone with Julie and tell her that if she came back to Arizona, they would buy her a horse or a piano. As I talked to Julie, Dad and Lynne would whisper in my other ear what to tell Julie. The horse promise worked, and she returned to Arizona to join us. Julie never got the horse, though.

We didn't see a whole lot of Dad when we lived in Arizona, especially during the school year. Dad was working at JD's every night but Mondays and then would stay out with friends even later. He'd come home early in the morning and sleep. In the summertime, we'd see him for a few hours after he woke up. We'd go out for dinner each week on Dad's night off.

Dad would knock over his glass of tea almost every time we ate out. I thought he was clumsy; he was actually on speed, taking pills like white crosses and black mollies. We never knew he was taking pills when we were kids and didn't know enough about drugs to suspect anything.

Dad's following really started to increase during his time at JD's. That was both good and bad. One night a guy came into the club threatening to shoot my dad because Dad had been messing around with the guy's wife. They snuck Dad out of the place, because everything but him was replaceable. Without Dad, the whole machine would have stopped.

While Dad was escaping, some of the guys talked to the angry man, trying to settle him down. When he realized that Dad had departed, he ran out and took off in his car. The police caught him down the road and arrested him.

An overly obsessive fan also started following Dad at JD's. She believed that she had been married to my dad in a previous life and claimed that if Dad recorded on yellow vinyl albums, all diseases known to man would be cured.

When Buddy was in kindergarten, the woman showed up at school one day, found Buddy, and told him that Dad was shooting a TV show and wanted Buddy to be on the program with him. Buddy always wanted to be a star. Still does, in fact. When Dad's autobiography came out in 1996, he went through the book to count which of us kids had been mentioned the most.

The thought of being on TV made Buddy an easy kidnapping target. It didn't take long for the police to find the woman and bring Buddy back safely. Dad didn't want the woman to have to go to jail. Instead, she was placed into a mental hospital for a while.

That wasn't the last we heard of that woman, though. After she got out of the hospital, she would pop up from time to time. She even followed Dad to Nashville when he moved there. Sometime in 1978 or '79, the mail stopped coming to Dad's office. When the staff realized it, they called the post office, which informed them that Dad's wife had come in and requested that all his mail be forwarded to her address. Turned out "Dad's wife" was that fan. Well, that was a federal crime, and it removed Dad's wishes from the equation. The woman got locked up in a mental institution, and I don't know if she ever got out.

Outside Looking In

Dad was "discovered" at JD's. His first album, *JD's Waylon Jennings*, released in 1964, was sold only at the bar. On April 16, 1964, he signed with A&M Records, owned by Herb Alpert and Jerry Moss, which initially released only a few of Dad's singles. RCA recording artist Bobby Bare heard Dad's song "Four Strong Winds"—which was a single that A&M released—and called RCA Records president Chet Atkins to tell him that if he didn't sign my dad to a contract, he was crazy.

Bobby came by our house to talk to Dad about signing with RCA. Obviously, that was an important meeting, and Dad told Julie, Buddy, and me that it was imperative that we be on our best behavior.

"You can meet the guy," he told us, "and then go to your rooms and let us do business."

Julie, Buddy, and I went into the bedroom that Buddy and I shared. From our window, we could see out front to where this man coming to see Dad would drive up in his car.

"Who's coming over?" Buddy asked.

"Bobby Bare," I answered.

"Who's that?"

"You know Captain Kangaroo? The Dancing Bear?" I asked Buddy.

He nodded.

"That's him."

Buddy got all excited, and when a car pulled up to our house, he watched as Bobby Bare—not Dancing Bear—stepped out.

Buddy freaked out and started running around the house, screaming and crying. Julie pointed at me and yelled to Dad, "It was him! It was him!"

Bobby Bare came to the front door right in the middle of all the commotion. Dad, equal parts pissed and embarrassed, tried to settle us down as his guest came inside. Bobby got a kick out of it. It took Dad a little longer to see the humor in the situation, aided by the fact that the meeting led to Atkins offering Dad a record contract. Dad was still under contract to A&M, but he worked out a deal under which he would give A&M all his publishing works for one year. Dad signed with Atkins and RCA in 1965 and wrote songs for RCA under the pseudonym "Jackson King" until his deal with A&M ended.

From his success at JD's, Dad earned more money, which allowed us to move to a bigger house in Scottsdale when I was in fourth grade.

Lynne made us stay outside when Dad was away from the house; we could only come inside when she told us to. It was hot in Scottsdale, but Lynne wouldn't let us into the house unless we proved to her that we had to go to the bathroom. She was the stereotypical mean stepmom, and it took me a long, long time and a lot of praying to Jesus to forgive her.

A man who lived down the street noticed that we were outside all the time, and he talked Lynne and Dad into letting me join the Boys Club. He was a nice man who collected rocks and taught me how to make jewelry and how to use a hacksaw to make puzzle boxes.

When Lynne did allow us inside, we were required to stay off the carpeted areas until bedtime. The living room was carpeted, so we never could go into that room. Dad never knew about Lynne's rule; he was oblivious to a lot of things, partly because of how much he was gone, yet also by choice.

The times when Dad was with us, he was a wonderful dad. He played with us and spent time with us. We got along great with Dad. He was never the one to provide physical correction when needed, because he didn't believe in corporal punishment and wouldn't allow the schools to physically punish us. When it came to discipline at home, he preferred to correct us verbally and send us to our rooms. He wasn't harsh unless we pushed him too far. But when he was mad, he could give us a talking to that made us wish he'd beat us instead.

The serious discipline was left to Momma and Grandma before we moved to Arizona, and then it became my job to keep Julie and Buddy in line.

Julie was strong headed and didn't like me telling her what to do; she wanted to be the oldest so she could be the one giving orders. If Julie got into trouble, I got into trouble for not doing my job. Julie was responsible for Buddy, and he was scared of her. If Julie told Buddy not to do something, he wouldn't. For the most part, Buddy was quiet and minded his own business. When Buddy did do something wrong, Julie got in trouble and then I got in trouble. The best thing for the three of us was for none of us to cause any problems.

I hate to admit it, but I could be mean as a kid. The only girl I ever hit was my sister. I would hit Julie in the middle of the back with a raised knuckle. Once I discovered that girls were different from guys, I quit doing that.

Lynne liked to bet the greyhounds. She had a guy friend who drove a Model A Ford, and he'd come over when Dad was working or sleeping, and he and Lynne would figure out what to bet at the dog races.

I was a sneaky little guy, and late one night when I was nine, Lynne and this guy were planning their bets. I slipped into the sunken living room and hid behind some plants. I heard Lynne and the man talking about some things she wouldn't have wanted me to hear. They were talking bad about Dad and about how they were screwing each other when he wasn't around.

The next day, I called either Grandma or Uncle Tommy—I think it was Grandma—and reported what I had heard and how Lynne had been treating us. Dad got pissed—not so much because Lynne was screwing around on him, but about what she had been doing to us kids.

A week later, Dad took Julie and me out for a car ride. He offered each of us a stick of Wrigley's Spearmint gum and then told us that he would be divorcing Lynne.

That was right before Christmas, and Dad came into the house one day and announced that he had bought Momma a new house and that Uncle Tommy was coming to get us and take us back to Texas to live with her.

"So go down into the living room and open your toys," Dad told us.

"They can't go in there," Lynne said. "They'll mess up the furniture."

We darted toward the living room—early Christmas gifts *and* uncharted territory!—and Dad didn't try to stop us.

We started ripping off the wrapping paper while Lynne was going nuts over us being in her living room. When we had opened all our gifts, Dad ordered, "Jump on those couches!"

6

PAINFUL LOSS

The house Dad bought us was one block from Aunt Squawky's and in a nice neighborhood in Irving. Too bad our stay there was short.

Our new home had three bedrooms. Buddy and I shared one, Julie and Deana shared one, and Mom had her own. The house payment was made from Arizona, where Dad and Lynne were in the process of splitting up. One day Momma showed me a check from Dad for $200.

"I'm supposed to get one every two weeks, and I'm going to show it to you," she told me. "If I didn't show it to you, we didn't get one."

I don't know if the checks kept coming, but she didn't show me another one after that. Whether Dad was sending the checks or not, Mom said she couldn't afford the house anymore, and she moved us to another neighborhood in Irving that was pretty much a ghetto.

Mom worked at a drive-in joint that served burgers,

sandwiches, beer, Coke, and Dr Pepper. She would drop us off at the movie theater sometimes when she couldn't find, or afford, a babysitter, and we would stay at the theater all day while she worked. That was how I saw *Nashville Rebel* for the first time after it came out in 1966.

Dad wasn't doing much touring at the time. Lucky Moeller, Dad's booking agent, told him that producers were casting for the movie and that he would be perfect for the role of Arlin Grove, a young man recently released from the Army whose pursuit of a country music career takes him all the way to the Grand Ole Opry. That was the only movie in which Dad was the lead actor.

I thought it was going to be cool to watch my dad in a movie. Then as the opening credits rolled, Dad was hitchhiking, caught a ride, and got beat up in a fight. *That ain't right,* I remember thinking. *They're beating the crap out of Dad!*

By this point, Dad was traveling back and forth a lot between Arizona—where he was still playing JD's—and Nashville. When Dad did a show near us, he'd stop by and see us. The first time he came to Irving after we had moved back to live with Mom, he brought Johnny Cash with him; they were part of a package tour. When they arrived at the house Dad had bought for Mom, we weren't there. Dad went over to Aunt Squawky's, and she gave Dad directions to our new, new home.

Imagine Dad bringing Cash to introduce him to his kids and ex-wife, and the address he was given took him to a cheap duplex in the ghetto.

Thus, Dad was already perturbed when he entered the

house. Then he noticed there wasn't a TV in the living room. The TV was in my room because I watched the most TV in the family and I had rolled it out of the living room, but Dad didn't know we did have a TV. Then when Dad laid eyes on us, we had been playing in puddles and had those little scabs you get on your legs when you're splashing around in dirty water. We had to look rather pitiful.

Dad flipped out.

Those were the circumstances under which I met Johnny. Except I didn't make the connection that it was Johnny Cash the extremely famous singer. As far as I knew, he was just another friend of my dad's.

He and Dad looked a lot alike back then, especially the way they slicked back their hair. When the movie *The Road to Nashville* came out and showcased a bunch of country artists, including Dad and Cash, I saw the movie poster from a distance and thought my dad was on there. When I walked closer, I noticed I had mistaken Cash for my own dad.

Dad still had a contract with JD's, but JD's granted him leeway so he could miss nights in order to go to Nashville. The time came in 1966, though, for Dad to move to Nashville and make that his permanent home and recording base.

Dad was still in the process of divorcing Lynne, and he had a wife-in-waiting named Barbara Rood who moved to Nashville with him. They were trying to keep their relationship secret. Dad was on the verge of going big, but he wasn't there yet and couldn't afford his own place in Nashville. He and Barbara stayed at various motels/hotels until Cash decided to get a place in Nashville for when he was there. He and Dad moved in together at the Fountain Bleu apartments in Madison, just north of Nashville. Barbara rented an apartment in the same place.

Neither Dad nor Cash could remember their keys, so they were constantly locking themselves out and would have to kick their door in to get inside. The apartment manager got fed up with them and replaced their door with one that swung out instead of in. Dad was the first to come home without his keys and took a big kick at the new door. When he told me about his introduction to the door, he said that every bone in his body had jarred.

Dad and Cash both had drug habits. One time Cash ran out of drugs. Dad had bought a nice Cadillac, and Johnny was convinced that Dad kept some drugs behind the glove compartment. Cash disassembled the whole area around the glove compartment looking for drugs that weren't there. Not only did he come up empty on his search, but he also had to pay to have Dad's torn-up dash repaired.

After Dad and Lynne's divorce came through, he married Barbara. She was a blond, blue-eyed beauty queen from a family of money; her father had invented a mechanical cotton picker. Barbara had attended college, was smart, and handled the books for Dad.

They were married less than a year, though.

The road life just wasn't for Barbara, and her father offered to pay my dad $100,000 per year and buy them a house if he would stay married to Barbara. Dad wouldn't even have to work a job—just stay home and make Barbara happy. But that would have meant giving up his music career because he wouldn't be free to travel.

Dad's response to Barbara's father: "Well, I think me and your daughter need to get a divorce."

I didn't get to know Barbara well. I liked Barbara during the limited time I was around her. I think Dad liked her, too. One time, Dad brought Barbara when he came to see us in the ghetto and they took us to the Fort Worth Zoo. On another occasion, in Littlefield, Dad and Barbara took Julie and me out to eat at the local Dairy Cream where Grandma's sister, Aunt Lucille, worked.

Barbara leaned over to Julie and said, "I want to tell you one thing: There's nothing a man can do that a woman can't do, and don't let no man or woman tell you any different."

Dad leaned over to me and said, making sure Barbara and Julie could hear him, "Ask one of them to piss into a Coke bottle without getting it on the side."

Dad and I laughed.

"You got me on that one," Barbara conceded.

Restored Relationship

Grandpa Jennings died following a heart attack on June 3, 1968, when I was eleven and living in Littlefield. He was fifty-three and hadn't been sick. It was completely unexpected. Grandpa was a big, heavy man, but it was mostly muscle. He was built like an oak barrel and was as solid as one, too.

Julie, Buddy, and I had gone to the swimming pool at the end of the street where we lived and were walking back to Grandma and Grandpa's house. They owned a yellow Impala, and it was sitting empty in the middle of the street with all four doors open. We walked into the house and no one was there.

My best friend, Buddy Jungman, lived across the street, and he told me that an ambulance had come to take Grandpa to the hospital.

Grandpa had heartburn a lot, and his remedy was baking soda. He'd put a teaspoon in his mouth, drink a glass of water, and lie on his stomach over a bed or a chair until he belched. On that particular day, he had bent over a chair and suffered a heart attack. They called an ambulance and decided before it arrived to drive Grandpa to the hospital themselves and helped him to the Impala. Just as they pulled into the street, the ambulance showed up and they transferred Grandpa from the car to the ambulance.

Grandpa never came home.

Dad was in Toronto when Grandpa passed. He was still with Barbara at the time, and they came as soon as they could to be with the family.

My uncle Bo, who was thirteen, had a difficult time dealing with Grandpa's death. One day, he took the car and ran off. Dad asked where Bo had gone. I said I didn't know, and Dad said, "Let's go find him." Littlefield's a small town, and we were able to track him down at a friend's house.

Dad took Grandpa's death pretty hard, too. Grandpa was the glue that held the entire family together, and he and Dad had experienced some rough patches in their relationship that started when Dad divorced my mom. In the Church of Christ, you just didn't get divorced. Then Dad got divorced again, from Lynne. The first one had already been one too many for Grandpa.

Dad and Grandpa stopped talking to each other for a while, and it had nothing to do with Dad's music or his destructive lifestyle. Actually, at that time, nobody in the family knew that Dad was on pills. They just suspected he was hyperactive.

As far as Grandma was concerned, Dad could do no wrong. She didn't approve of his divorces, but nothing ever changed in their relationship. Grandma was the type of person who tried to smooth things over, and she continued talking to Dad like nothing had happened. I think even though Dad's divorces went against her beliefs, she didn't let it affect her relationship with him because she wanted to try to bring him back to the light.

Sometimes we could sense tension between Dad and Grandpa, but whatever they were feeling toward each other went unsaid, at least in front of the rest of us.

We would all eat together when Dad visited. When there was no dessert, Grandpa would mix sorghum syrup and butter and smash it up with a fork. Then he'd sop it up with bread and eat it. After he'd finished, he would slide his chair to the far side of the kitchen, lean against the wall on the back legs of the chair, and eat ice from his glass of tea. Dad would pull out his guitar and play his latest recording when he had a new release out. Other times, he would pick a tune that he was thinking about recording.

Their relationship turned good again when *Nashville Rebel* made its premiere at the Palace Theatre in Littlefield.

The family and the townsfolk had thought Dad was a little nuts for trying to support a family by playing the guitar and singing. Dad hadn't made much money to that point, so it was easy to understand their second-guessing.

But when those people, including Grandpa, saw Dad for the first time performing his music on the movie screen, I think they began to reconsider their assessment.

Grandpa went into the theater bathroom after the movie, and some guy was making positive remarks about my dad. Grandpa, who didn't talk much to begin with, told the guy, "Yeah, that's my son."

Seeing Dad in the movie and hearing the local man talk nice about my dad made Grandpa real proud. It wasn't like the movie made Grandpa think, *My son's a star, I'm going to like him again*. My dad had been working hard and had sacrificed a lot, including family time, to make it in the music business. He had paid his dues. When someone says my dad was an overnight sensation, I contend he was a fifteen-year overnight sensation. I think after seeing *Nashville Rebel*, Grandpa recognized that Dad had made the right choice after all and decided that it was time to give him a break.

Dad and Grandpa started talking again, and their relationship got back to like it had been before the divorce with Momma. I think the Good Lord had something to do with bringing Dad and Grandpa back together, and I'm grateful that He did, because it was just a couple of years later that Grandpa died.

I can't imagine how Dad would have responded if he and his dad hadn't been on good terms when Grandpa died. It was hard enough on him as it was. Dad loved Grandpa—always did, even when they weren't talking to each other. Dad felt like he had let his dad down, and he wanted more time with Grandpa to try to make it up to him.

Dad refused to go see Grandpa's body before the funeral because he wanted to remember him the way he was the last time he'd seen him alive. But Dad did look at Grandpa in the casket at the funeral, and that was rough for him. Dad didn't like the way Grandpa looked. He looked like a facsimile of Grandpa. He didn't look strong. He looked, well, *dead*.

"When I die," Dad told me at the funeral, "I don't want no open casket."

A Deal's a Deal

Grandma turned to drinking after the funeral. She had drunk very little, if any, before Grandpa passed.

There was a couch on Grandma and Grandpa's back porch where we would sit and smoke our cigarettes and shoot our BB guns. The doctor who had delivered me lived across the alley, and he had a rooster wind vane that we would shoot and make spin. "I brought you into this world," he'd remind me, "and I can take you out." I also stole grapes from his garden. "I was the first to whoop your butt, and I can whoop it now," he'd say.

That back porch was a gathering spot for our family, and Grandma started hiding her drinking bottle behind that couch. She didn't hide it very well, though, because we could see it.

One night in the first couple of months after Grandpa had died, she got really drunk. She was hurting, missing Grandpa in a bad way. Bo was trying to console her, and Julie and I overheard her tell Bo, "It's those kids' fault. If they weren't here, he'd still be alive." We knew better than to accept that we had caused Grandpa's death, or that Grandma actually believed that we did, but it still was shocking to hear her state that.

Buddy, who was eight, could make friends with anyone. When we'd lived in Arizona, he would walk up and down the streets and talk to strangers as though they had known each other for years. Buddy made friends in Littlefield with a man named James. He brought James to the house to meet Grandma, and James and Grandma took a liking to each other. They started dating and made plans to get married, sell the house, buy a motor home, and see America.

After I finished the seventh grade, Grandma told us we would be going back to live with Momma in Irving.

I wasn't happy about that because Mom drank. When I was around Mom, I had to be the man of the house. At my grandparents', I had been able to be a regular kid. Grandma would take us out to get ice cream or a burger. That didn't happen much at my mom's house.

Shortly after she informed us that we would be moving, I walked into Grandma's bedroom one day and saw a piece of paper with "Waylon" and a phone number and room number written on it. I called the number and asked for the room number.

Dad answered.

"This is Terry," I told him.

His reply was rather sharp. "What do you want?" His tone caught me by surprise.

"I don't want nothing," I answered.

"If you don't want nothing, you wouldn't have called."

"No," I explained, "there was this number lying here on Grandma's nightstand, and I called you."

Dad relaxed when he heard that.

"So there's nobody there with you now?" he asked.

"No," I told him. "They went to Dairy Queen to get a hamburger and ice cream."

I then told Dad how we were going to live with Mom by the next school year and that I didn't like that. "I want to live with you," I told him.

"Here's the deal," Dad said. "Give me thirty days and I'll work it out so that you don't have to live with your momma. You can live with me."

"That's great!" I told him, and we said our good-byes.

The others came back from Dairy Queen, and I was all happy. That raised their curiosity.

"Dad told me that in thirty days," I told them, "I could live with him."

They didn't believe me.

When it came time for us to leave to go live with Mom, I told Grandma, "I'm waiting my thirty days."

Grandma got on the phone with Dad and confirmed our deal. Julie and Buddy left to live with Momma and Deana. Now thirteen, I stayed behind to wait for my dad to arrange for me to move to Nashville.

7

FUN-LOVING JESSI

When it came to marrying, the fourth time was the charm for Dad.

At the time when I was waiting for Dad to make arrangements for me to join him in Nashville, he was with Jessi Colter, who had a daughter named Jennifer.

Jessi was a country singer and songwriter. Dad's brother Tommy introduced him to Jessi at JD's, when Dad was married to Barbara and Jessi was married to rock-and-roll guitarist Duane Eddy. Dad and Barbara's divorce came soon after he met Jessi, and he and Jessi started seeing each other.

I had met Jessi before they married, and I immediately liked her. Jessi was younger than my dad's other wives—she was only fourteen years older than me—and the prettiest thing I'd seen outside of my mom. Although Jessi didn't talk a lot, she made an effort to have fun with us kids. I think she was out of her element a little bit with us kids, though. We West Texas tornadoes in blue jeans were a different breed of animal than she was used to.

Just as he promised, Dad came to Littlefield and picked me up to take me on a two-week vacation with Jessi and his band in his touring bus. Dad had an all-black bus that originally belonged to Cash. Even the bumpers were painted black. We called that bus the Black Mariah, and it could get hot inside that all-black thing. The back of the bus had a sleeping area for Dad and Jessi. The middle section was supposed to be a kitchen, but it was used for storing equipment. The rest of us hung out in the front.

I remember on our way to Arizona, the bus got a flat tire. We couldn't get the wheel jacked up high enough to get the tire off, so Dad got out there with a claw hammer and beat the asphalt out from underneath the tire. Dad was sweating to death with that sun bouncing off the asphalt. There wasn't water on the bus, and Jessi and Sonny Ray, who played a two-neck guitar, took empty cartons over to a horse trough by a windmill and filled them with water for Dad and the rest of us.

Jessi was cool. She bought me some new clothes on that trip. Except they weren't exactly the type of clothes we wore in West Texas. The shirt was a yellow gauzelike material with really puffy sleeves, like the sleeves of a pirate's shirt. The pants were orange-and-white plaid jeans. Perhaps those would have been hip in Los Angeles, but not in Littlefield.

A couple of months after that vacation, I went back out to Arizona with Grandma, Julie, Buddy, and Bo to meet up with Dad and Jessi. We were in a small banquet room in a hotel for a dinner that Jessi had catered in. The first item they served us was shrimp cocktail. Bo and I looked at each other like, *What's that?!?* We touched the food and it was cold. We thought it might be a dessert, although it didn't look like ice cream. Dad was sitting off to the side trying not to laugh at us. Finally, we both built up the nerve to give the shrimp cocktail a taste test. That was when we confirmed it definitely was not ice cream.

The next course was split pea soup. Bo and I weren't going to touch anything that kind of green, and we knew there was no need to discuss trying the soup. Next was salad. That, we were familiar with. We ate the salad.

The main course followed: rack of lamb, and it was *red*. We were taught growing up that if pork, beef, or any other meat was red, we shouldn't eat it. To this day, I still order my steaks well done. Bo and I looked at that bloody meat, and there was no way we were going to eat that. Instead, we picked at the vegetables around the lamb. Fortunately, there was cake for dessert.

As we were leaving, Jessi was disappointed that our family had eaten so little of the food. Dad told her, "You don't serve sheep to a bunch of cowboys."

When we got into the car, Dad told us, "I know you're hungry. Let's go to a burger joint." We would have voted for a burger and fries over rack of lamb and split pea soup any day of the week.

Pretty-boy clothes and rack of lamb aside, I was excited about getting to live with Dad, Jessi, and Jennifer in Nashville.

After I had moved to Nashville, Jessi set up a birthday party for Dad. We boarded the *Belle Carol* riverboat for a cruise down the Cumberland River. A who's who of the town were in attendance, including the Hee Haw Honeys from *Hee Haw*. Dad introduced me to Lisa Todd, who played the character Sunshine Cornsilk. She was beautiful and well-endowed. She also was tall, and I was thirteen. When Lisa Todd hugged me, my face was buried in heaven.

Dad said all his pleasantries to the guests and blew out the candles on his cake. Right before we were to take off, Dad jumped off the boat to do who knew what. We were all stuck on the boat without him for two hours.

The summer before my eighth-grade year, we went out to Los Angeles when Dad's *The Taker/Tulsa* album was released. We stayed on Sunset Boulevard at the Hyatt Regency, which was known as the Riot House because of all the rock stars who liked to stay there.

Jessi had gone to swim in the rooftop pool, and there was a knock on our door. I was wearing a pair of pants, no shirt, and no shoes when I opened the door and fell into shock at seeing Shelley Fabares standing in front of me. I'd had a crush on her since watching her on *The Donna Reed Show*. Jessi and Shelley had been roommates, and Shelley had come by to see her.

I said that Jessi was at the pool, and even though Shelley had to have been at that hotel dozens of times, I volunteered, "I'll show you where she is." So, I walked *the* Shelley Fabares to Jessi. It would be an exaggeration to say that my feet never touched the ground between our room and the pool, but I don't think they touched more than two or three times. At the pool, Jessi formally introduced us.

Shelley hung around the next day, too. Dad was playing at Knott's Berry Farm, and we all rode together. But then some man showed up to be with Shelley and crushed my dreams.

Giving Up Pot—Temporarily

Dad and Jessi married in 1969. Twice. The first time was in Las Vegas in a ceremony. The second time, which I didn't hear about until years later, was performed by Jessi's mom, a Pentecostal preacher.

When I moved in with Dad and Jessi, we lived in a condo in Bell Meade, southwest of Nashville. One of my first memories there is a breakfast when we were eating meat and eggs with flour tortillas instead of toast. Dad told me we ate tortillas because we couldn't afford bread.

"If there is something you don't like about this house, speak up and say it," he told me as we were eating. "The reason I'm telling you this is because we ran out of sugar one time, and Jessi decided to put molasses in my coffee. I didn't want to hurt her feelings, so I told her, 'This is good coffee, Jessi.' It was the worst-tasting coffee, but I told her it was good. And the coffee got worse every day. We could afford sugar, but Jessi thought I liked the molasses so much that she kept buying molasses. So if you don't like something, speak up or you'll be eating it for the rest of your life."

I started eighth grade at Bell Meade Junior High, and two weeks into the school year, Buddy and Julie moved in with us. I loved the three of us being together again, but that also meant I was back to having to keep the other two in line. I didn't like always having to be responsible for my brother and sister. Like I've said, Jessi was really cool. But in her partying days when she would go out with Dad, she'd have to sleep in after a long night, and I'd be the one who had to make sure the kids got to their buses on time.

During the eighth grade we moved to Donelson, which was clear over to the other side of Nashville. Buddy got bused to one school, and they bused me to Cameron Junior High, right in the middle of the projects.

I started drinking and smoking pot in Donelson, at age thirteen. I kept a matchbox full of seeds in my room. I don't know why; I can only guess I thought I'd plant them and see if I could grow my own weed.

Jessi was in my room one day and found the seeds. She took two and placed them in a bottle, and when Dad came home, she told him that I was smoking pot and that she had proof.

I was working at a carnival, selling ride tickets. Dad sent someone who worked for him to come to the carnival and order me to "get home—now." When I entered the house, Julie, Buddy, and Jennifer were downstairs with Dad and Jessi.

"I understand you have been smoking pot," Dad said.

Lying to my dad was not an option. Ever. If you lied to Dad, there would be hell to pay.

So I admitted that, yes, I had been smoking pot, and Dad gave me the biggest ass chewing I'd ever heard. He was cussing me out and telling me how bad drugs were and that if I ended up on drugs, I wouldn't be doing so as a part of his house.

"Now get in your room—you're grounded," he ended.

Dad scared me so much that I went to my room with my mind already made up that I'd never smoke pot again.

Dad left for his office downtown. A little later, the phone rang. Jessi answered and said the call was for me.

"Terry," Dad said on the other end, "I'm sorry, but I had to jump your ass in front of the other kids so they'd know I was serious. If you're gonna smoke pot, tell me and I'll get you a motel room to do it in. If you've got a girl, I'll get you a motel room. That way you don't have to do it around the house and get caught. I won't have to chew you out no more. I got nothin' against it. But don't tell Jessi. She has to believe you're in trouble."

Before we hung up, I had reversed my earlier decision to give up pot.

Not too long after receiving Dad's blessing to smoke weed, I went out with a friend and we got high. Dad was on the road and had taken Buddy with him, so only Jessi, Julie, and Jennifer were home. I had a bed and a couch in my room, and my friend and I were going to go to my house and crash.

"Look," I told my friend when we got home, "we're gonna go in the door, and you go straight down the hallway and go in the first room on the right. That's my bedroom. I'll tell them good night and then I'll be there."

My friend walked ahead of me, and I paused to say good night to Jessi, Julie, and Jennifer.

"What's this?" my friend yelled down the hallway.

I waved to my friend with my left hand, trying to get him to shush so our state of being high wouldn't be discovered.

I was accustomed to questions about my room. I had

painted the room and windows black, and another friend painted the universe on the walls in blacklight paint. I also had a half-played game of chess glued to the ceiling above my bed, and I would lie in bed and play out that game in my mind. I had a strange room, but it wasn't the paint or the universe or the ceiling chess game my friend was asking about.

Coat hangers were all over the floor. *Playboy* pictures had been stuck to the walls, with Band-Aids covering the parts that would have appealed most to a thirteen-year-old boy.

I didn't have a good answer for him.

"We're in the room, we're safe, and you're sleeping on the couch," I told him. Then I rolled into my bed and felt spaghetti at my feet and salt on my pillow. The girls sure must have been proud of themselves. But I was tired, high, and in no mood to acknowledge their prank. I retrieved a blanket from the closet, threw it on the bed and over the pillow, and went straight to sleep.

I woke up the next morning and put on a new pair of jeans to go to the bathroom across the hall. They had sewn the bottoms of the legs so I couldn't slide my feet through. I tossed those jeans aside and tried to slip on another pair. That pair had been sewn shut, too. So had the next pair I picked up. Really needing to go, I put on the jeans I'd worn the night before and opened my bedroom door to find new bedding, sodas, potato chips, milk balls, and chocolate kisses (my favorite candy) on the floor right outside the door.

My friend left and the girls said the items were a peace offering. They thought I was mad at them because I hadn't come back out of my room the night before.

"No," I told them. "I was tired and just went to bed."

I had to admit, though, they pulled off a pretty good prank.

Life with Jessi was fun, and that was good, because we never knew for sure how long Dad would be gone on a road trip. Lucky Moeller was Dad's booking agent then, and he liked to keep Dad busy. Dad was in demand, too. Clubs would call and ask for Dad to make an appearance, and Lucky would work out a contract and add the place onto Dad's tour.

There was no mapping when it came to scheduling shows; if Dad could drive there, he would play there. He'd play a Friday and Saturday somewhere for $2,000 to $2,500. Other artists would play the same places and draw smaller crowds and get paid the same. But, still, Dad loved to play so much that if he had a night open and could afford to, he'd stop at some bar and play a free show.

Dad formed a company called Utopia Productions, run by a guy named George Laeb, who had become Dad's new booking agent, and his office assistant, Marylou Hyatt. Over time, Dad's appearance fees rose to between $5,000 to $7,500 for two nights, and the club owners were willing to pay more because he filled the seats, and that meant more liquor sold.

Dad didn't become a national name through promotion or press coverage. He became popular by playing club after club, anywhere and everywhere. People knew who he was because he built a following by playing his butt off. The schedule was tough, and a one-month tour could turn into six months without coming home.

During one of those trips that went on much longer than originally planned, Jessi and us kids put up a big, beautiful

Christmas tree after Thanksgiving. Dad missed spending Christmas with us, and Jessi really wanted Dad to see our tree. So the tree stayed up.

Dad didn't get home until June, and he was greeted by a dead fire hazard in the living room with all the ornaments still on board.

"What is that?" Dad asked.

"That's our Christmas tree," I answered. "Jessi wanted us to save it so you could see it."

"I've seen it," he said. "Now get it out of here."

We took the decorations down and, in the middle of June, dragged our Christmas tree to the curb for the trash collectors to pick up. I'm sure they had a couple of questions they would have liked to ask us.

On a later tour, when I was on the crew, we were gone so long that when Dad and I pulled up to our home, no one was there. So we went to Dad's office, where we were informed that Jessi had moved. Dad asked for her phone number, and it had not changed.

Dad called her and asked, "Where do we live now?"

"I'm sorry," Jessi said. "I forgot to tell you I was moving."

"I thought you were trying to get rid of us," Dad told her.

Friction over Religion

Jessi hit me one time, and I deserved it. In fact, she probably should have hit me harder than she did.

When I was in eighth grade, she was getting ready to go

out for a special night or event with Dad. She had all her makeup on and she was looking pretty. She walked into the den/kitchen area, and I started squirting her in the face with a water gun. She told me to stop, and I didn't. I laughed, too, and she came up and slapped me. That made me stop.

While we were living in Donelson, Jessi's mother died. I had never met her mother, but I was a pallbearer at the funeral because one of the pallbearers got sick and couldn't make it. I also was a last-minute replacement pallbearer at Jessi's dad's funeral years later.

Jessi was awesome, and she never seemed like a stepmother to me. Not only did I like Jessi a lot, but I respected her. She was a great songwriter and singer, and she could have had a bigger career of her own. But she gave that up to support Dad and his career.

She changed her lifestyle after her mother passed away. Jessi put down her cigarettes and picked up the Bible. She had grown up in church and started attending church regularly again and cut out the partying. I was okay with everything but her stopping smoking, because it was her cigarettes that I'd been swiping.

Jessi's newfound spirituality caused a point of friction between her and my dad. She initially tried to push her religion on Dad, and he rejected it. He walked into the house once and Jessi and some of her church friends were trying to pray the devil out of one of the friends' little boy. "This shit ain't going on in my house," Dad told the group. "Get the f—— out of here. Do it in someone else's house, not mine."

I don't think Dad was rejecting religion in general, just

that kind. I think part of Dad's problem with some religion stemmed from churches that were too eager to get donations from him. They seemed more interested in what he could give them instead of him as a person.

Dad had kept his Black Mariah bus, which Cash had previously owned, for years. At one point, I took the big couch cushions from the bus and placed them in my bedroom to use as chairs and as an extra bed for friends. When the Hells Angels had started traveling with Dad and handling his merchandise, Dad let them use the Black Mariah. The windshield wiper motor went out on that bus, so they rigged up a rope to each blade and when it rained, two girls stood at the front of the bus and pulled the ropes to keep the windshield clear. That system worked surprisingly well.

Jessi asked Dad if he would donate that bus to her church so it could be used to pick up kids and bring them to church. Dad told her, "I'll take the top off that bus and make it into a planter before I give it to any damn church." A few years later, though, he changed his mind and donated the bus.

There were two occasions when Dad said he wanted to divorce Jessi. The first was around 1977, best I can recall. I know it was before 1979, because that was when my youngest brother, Waylon Albright Jennings—we call him Shooter— was born. Dad took me and Julie for a ride in the car and offered us a piece of Wrigley's Spearmint gum. The gum made me immediately flash back to the time when Dad told us he was divorcing Lynne.

Oh, crap. Here we go—we're moving back to Texas.

"I'm thinking about divorcing Jessi," Dad told us. "What do you think?"

"I don't get it," I said.

"What do you not get?" he asked. "I'm thinking about divorcing her."

"Why?" I asked him. "You have the best of both worlds here. She lets you do anything you want. She's taking care of the house. Who else is going to put up with your crap like she does?"

"You know, you're kinda right," Dad kinda admitted.

I was relieved. I don't know how Julie felt, because she had always held out hope that Dad would marry Momma again, and she gave all of Dad's wives a hard time. We knew the other women Dad was dating at the time and that any one of them could become our stepmother, and Jessi was clearly my pick over Dad's wives-in-waiting.

The possibility of divorce came up in another conversation in 1982, but without the spearmint gum. Dad was very serious the first time, but I don't think his mind was near as set the second time, and it was easy to convince him to stay with Jessi. I don't know why Dad would want to leave Jessi. Maybe there was some kind of clock inside Dad that would reach a point where he'd been with one wife for so long and he felt it was time to find a new one. (Even though he'd probably already found her.)

After Shooter was born—proving wrong Dad's assumption that he was too old to have another child—Jessi wanted my dad to get a vasectomy.

"What if my next wife wants kids?" he asked. I guess Dad always wanted to leave his options open.

Dad claimed that before he and Jessi married, Jessi wrote him a letter that said he was a wild stallion and needed someone who would let him run free. "You don't tame a wild stallion," Dad quoted Jessi writing.

I never read the letter. Jessi said she wrote it then recanted.

Years later, Dad was kind of defending himself to my wife, Debra, and told her, "You don't understand—Jessi begged me to marry her."

"No I didn't," Jessi chimed in.

Dad brought up the alleged letter and recited what it said. Jessi downplayed it.

"I took it to heart," Dad said. "That's why I had the freedom."

The reason Dad and Jessi stayed married until the day he died was that Jessi put up with his BS. I don't have a bad thing to say about Jessi. Fortunately, once Dad got sober, he was a different Waylon, and Jessi reaped the benefits of her enduring patience.

8

TROUBLE WITH THE LAW

The completion of my eighth-grade year brought another move for us—to a rental home in Mount Juliet, about twenty miles east of Nashville.

That was a dangerous house. The second-floor deck had not been completed, and if we walked outside through the kitchen door, we would have a long fall to the ground.

My dad arranged for me to keep going to school with my friends despite the move. A gigantic new high school—McGavock—had been built that combined Nashville's four high schools into one building. There were four principals in charge of the former north, south, east, and west schools, with one person over the entire school.

Dad and Jessi hired a housekeeper, whose husband happened to teach auto mechanics at McGavock. He would bring our housekeeper to the house in the morning and then I would ride with him to school.

That school was chaotic. It was the first year and they had

combined the schools, so they were trying to figure out a lot of things. We really didn't have to go to class at that school. If we showed up at homeroom, we would be considered in attendance for the day and receive a C average. Of course, we took advantage to arrange the occasional skip day after homeroom. There was a well house at a nearby creek, and some friends and I would hide out in that well house and discuss whether we should return to school. More often than not, we voted not to.

I had signed up for auto mechanics class the last period of the day. Needless to say, when I didn't show up for the last class some days and the teacher was my ride home and his wife was our housekeeper, it didn't take long for word to reach home that I was skipping school.

My punishment was being separated from my friends at McGavock and transferred to a school in Mount Juliet. I didn't fit in well at my new school. The students there were pretty redneck, and I had really long hair. I hated getting my hair cut because when we had lived with Grandma, she had cut our hair with these manual things that worked like shears. I've yet to see a barber use them in a professional shop.

Grandma had used the same "shears" on Dad, Tommy, James D., and then Bo, so by the time we came along, it was more like getting our hair pulled out instead of cut. Grandma gave us burr haircuts. *Burr* is too complimentary, really. Instead of a hairstyle, per se, we escaped Grandma's chair with stubbles on our heads.

When I was living with Dad and Jessi, he told me one day that I needed a haircut.

"Do I have to?" I asked him.

"Not if you don't want to," he said.

From that point, I'd only get the dead ends trimmed every once in a while. By the time I enrolled in Mount Juliet, my hair was down to the middle of my back. That put a big, fat target on me as far as the rednecks were concerned.

I signed up for auto mechanics class there, too, and a few days in, someone came up behind me and knocked me out with a crescent wrench. I didn't need a blow to the head to tell me that I didn't fit it at my new school, but the message came through loud and clear anyway.

I did make friends with a couple of girls who told me they had $2,000 and were running away from home. They asked if I wanted to join them. My decision-making process consisted of this: *Two girls and $2,000? Yeah, I'm in!*

The girls wanted to head to Texas, and we got as far as Bucksnort, Tennessee, about eighty miles down the road. In Bucksnort, we stopped at a minimarket truck stop, where we met a couple of hippie musicians named Homer and Jethro. They were carpenters building an A-frame log cabin, and we helped them install insulation. They were living in a treehouse while working on the cabin, and we stayed with them for three days. They said they had to go to Nashville, and we accompanied them. In wild coincidence, Dad's office was five blocks from where we stayed.

The girls and I scrapped the Texas idea and headed east instead, to Knoxville. There, the money ran out and we returned to Nashville after two weeks on the road.

Uncle Tommy, who had moved to Nashville when Dad

moved there, had been looking for me. Everyone was excited—and surprised—to see me when I walked into the house. They thought I was trying to pull a Jeremiah Johnson, the lead character (played by Robert Redford) in a movie of the same name in which a man decides to live as a mountain man.

They wanted to know what they had done wrong. I told them they hadn't done anything. They assumed I had run away from home. Heck, that wasn't what happened; I had just gone off to have some fun with two girls who had $2,000 they wanted me to help them spend.

Dad and Jessi to the Rescue

We had a pool table in the basement, and for Bud's birthday, we wanted to get him new cue sticks. After Jessi's mother had died, Jessi kept the El Torino that she had bought for her. Jessi told me to take the car and a friend to drive into downtown and buy cue sticks for Bud.

My friend and I had taken two quaaludes, and we had to hurry to get back in time for Bud's birthday celebration. I found a parking spot on Second Avenue. My friend and I took off running for the store, and I lost my balance on a small dip in the concrete and sprained my ankle. We continued on to buy the cue sticks and with my ankle throbbing, I told my friend to drive.

It started drizzling on our way home, plus the pills were starting to take effect. The car slid off the road and into the edge of a lake. The motor was still running, and neither of us was hurt.

"Just back it up," I told my friend. "We need to get these cues home."

He shifted into reverse, but the car didn't budge.

Located across the street was a small market where Jessi often sent me to pick up groceries. We climbed up the bank and went to the market to call the house and report what had happened. My ankle was still hurting pretty bad, so I sat on the curb of the parking lot to wait for Dad and Jessi. A policeman arrived before they did.

"Whose car is that?" he asked.

"Mine," I answered.

"Stand up," the cop told me.

When I stood, I put too much weight on the sprained ankle and pain ripped through my entire body. I fell over and knocked over a bunch of soda bottles stacked in front of the store.

The policeman arrested me for public drunkenness. Dad and Jessi had to come to the jail to bail me out. They believed me when I said that I wasn't drunk, and they took me to a doctor for a blood test to prove there was no alcohol in my system.

I wasn't going to cut my long hair for my court appearance, so the day we were supposed to go in front of the judge, Jessi pinned my hair up and put a short wig on me. In the courtroom, the policeman looked at me like, *That's not the guy I arrested*.

The judge read the charges against me and read from the officer's report that cited my fall and knocking over the bottles as his reason for arresting me. Jessi stood up and told the judge, "You've gotta know these Jennings men. They trip over a stripe in the road."

"Excuse me, Your Honor," my dad stood and said. "Do you do divorces, too? I might need one after this."

Dad and Jessi presented the blood test as our proof that there was no alcohol in my system at the time of the accident. The judge asked if I was drunk that day, and I truthfully answered, "No, sir. I wasn't drunk."

The judge declared me not guilty and dismissed us.

In the hallway outside the courtroom, I removed the wig and let my hair down. The cop was walking by at that time, and seeing I had covered my hair made him mad, he shook his head and stormed off.

On the Road with Dad

After the ninth grade, I'd had enough of school and dropped out. It wasn't a big deal with my parents. I didn't talk to Mom about it beforehand. I was talking with her on the phone only every once in a while, and bringing up Mom around Dad wasn't a good thing.

Dad had no problem with me dropping out, because school just hadn't been my thing. Dad had been called into a meeting with the principal after I had gotten caught smoking in the restroom, and the principal thought I needed a haircut. Dad brought Johnna Yursic, his road manager, with him. The meeting didn't really resolve anything. I didn't get in trouble for the smoking and didn't have to get a haircut. As we were leaving the principal's office, Johnna opened up his briefcase to show the principal a tape recorder that had been recording the meeting. Obviously, Dad had issues with the school system.

When I dropped out, Dad offered me a chance to go out to sell T-shirts and other merchandise at his shows, so I hit the road full-time with Dad for the first time.

We averaged about four shows per week, and it was common to drive 500 to 750 miles between shows. Dad supplied hotel rooms for the band and crew. Sometimes I roomed alone, and other nights I shared a room with the other merch guy. The band and crew were generally friendly and accepting of me, and I had a good time learning how much went into making Dad's shows happen.

I kept that job for only three or four months, though. I became too much of a tourist attraction, of sorts, because show promotors would announce from the stage, "You can buy T-shirts and albums out front, and as a matter of fact, Waylon's son is out there selling them." I had so many people wanting to ask questions about my dad and pose for photos with me that it made it difficult to do my job. I've always shied away from that kind of attention, because it makes me uncomfortable, and it was a nuisance having people know who I was.

There also was a T-shirt guy who caused problems for me. Technically, he was my boss, and he would give me the money from the merch sales in an envelope at the end of the night. But somehow the money would end up short or missing. One time I had the money and was in my hotel room, and he sent this girl down to knock on my door and tell me that he wanted the money. I kind of stammered for a second and said, "I don't know." Then I looked down the hall and he waved at me and said, "It's okay." I gave her the money, and she returned to his room.

When we were loading the bus to leave, he asked me, "Where's the money?"

"I gave it to the girl to give to you," I replied.

"I didn't send her down there to get no money," he said.

No girl, no money, it was gone. Terry's fault.

Another time, I put the money in my back pocket and went into the bathroom on the bus to smoke a joint. I sat the money on the sink and forgot it. I went back to the bathroom and, of course, it was gone. I brought it up before the bus stopped for a reason. The guys on the bus were trying to convince me that it probably slid down between the sink and the wall. But had that been the case, the envelope would have fallen into the storage bays under the bus. It wasn't there, and the money was never found.

I got tired of the problems that guy was causing me and with all the people bugging me while I was trying to sell merch, so I quit. Dad and Johnna Yursic tried to talk me into staying with them.

I said, "Naw, it ain't gonna happen."

"Why not?" Yursic asked.

"I don't like working with him, and he's stealing money," I told them of the other T-shirt guy.

"He ain't stealing money," Dad countered.

"Go read your road reports, and pay attention to the

miscellaneous expenses," I told him. "I don't understand how you can have miscellaneous expenses of $2,000 a day."

They looked at the reports, and sure enough, I was right. They fired the guy.

Bo and the "Stolen" Car

After the school year, Julie and I went to visit Mom in Texas. She had moved to Grand Prairie, not far from Irving, and we stayed there for two weeks while Buddy remained in Nashville. Jessi mailed us a letter saying that she and Dad had talked and decided it would be better for us to live with Mom because we didn't know how to act around rich people.

Julie got mad, partly because she wanted it to be *her* idea, not someone else's. Even though I liked living with Dad and Jessi, the letter didn't bother me too much. Pot cost fifteen dollars an ounce in Nashville and only ten bucks in Dallas. *Better price, better place*, I reasoned. I didn't want to hurt Dad's feelings, so I was okay with the move.

Bo needed to make a trip to Littlefield, and without telling Dad or Jessi, he drove the same El Torino that had belonged to Jessi's mother.

You could say Bo stole the car—there's a bit of a gray area there.

Dad called me and asked, "Do you have a car?"

"No, I don't."

"Well, Bo stole Jessi's momma's car," he told me. "It's in Littlefield. I've called James D. and told him to tell Bo to take the car to the service station James D. owns. James D.'s gonna service it, and if you can make it to Littlefield, the car's yours."

I hitchhiked with a friend to Littlefield, and my friend immediately caught a bus back to his home. James D. needed a couple of more days to work on the car. When he finished, I took off in the car for home with Julie, who happened to be visiting in Littlefield at the time. As the proverbial crow flies, it was less than a mile to where we were staying with Momma. But to drive there required following a more round-about route.

The car quit on the way home. Quit dead. It wouldn't come close to starting. It was the middle of the night, and we didn't want to walk the long way home, so we slept in the car. The next morning, we locked the car and walked through people's yards—in the daylight, when we wouldn't get shot—to get home. My stepfather, Wesley "Cotton" Hines, towed the car to the house, and I worked on the car and changed a lot of parts, but I couldn't fix it.

The car sat unused beside the driveway until I made a trip to Nashville. I had been living with Mom for about ten months, and Dad had been trying to talk me into moving back to Nashville. I committed to visiting for two weeks and told Dad that if I liked what I saw there, I'd come back to Grand Prairie, pack up my belongings, and move back in with him and Jessi.

In Texas I had been running with a new bunch of guys. One was called Cat because he was a cat burglar. Cat and his friends liked to "shop" at a parts store, buy mag tires, and stuff things into the wheel walls. All the time, they'd be casing the joint for later. I never got into stealing things with them, because I was too scared of getting caught. But I did hang around them because they could get their hands on really good pot.

Some of the guys owned a gas station, and before my visit to Nashville, I asked if they could fix my car while I was gone. I told them I'd give them $200, and if they needed more, I'd pay the balance when I came back home.

My trip to Nashville turned into a three-week visit. I decided I would move back to Dad and Jessi's and returned to Texas to pack up. When I went to the gas station to pick up my car, the place was empty and my car was nowhere to be seen.

I called Dad and told him, and he accused me of being in cahoots with the guys. Dad had the car parts traced and discovered that my buddies had stripped the car and sold the parts to a bunch of different places. Dad told me that my friends were headed to jail.

"Fine," I told him. "They stole the car, and they deserve to go to jail."

"Yeah, right," Dad said. "Like you didn't know they were going to do that."

I was finally able to convince Dad that I had no part in what had happened to the car.

The insurance company sent a check for $2,000 to cover the dismantled car. Dad told me to get with his bus driver, Thomas Terrell, who was from Georgia and knew a lot of used car dealers there. "Rugus," as we called him, said he could get me a great deal, and he and I drove from Nashville to Georgia to car-shop. Rugus helped me buy a yellow Dodge Challenger for $2,000.

Well, about three months later, the transmission went out on the Challenger, and I had to put it in a shop. My friend Kevin Mansfield and I stopped by the garage to check the status. It was pouring rain, and we pulled up under the cover to take a look. We looked into the garage and the car was still up on a jack. And the rain had caused the roof of the building to cave in on top of my car. My Challenger was done.

At least it was a little easier to convince my dad that I hadn't had anything to do with that incident.

9

THE OUTLAWS

Dad referred to Chet Atkins as "God."

Chet, the most respected guitar player and producer in Nashville at the time, ran RCA's Nashville operations. Dad said, "When Chet calls you and offers you a record deal, it's like God offering you a record deal."

Any artist who had Chet's stamp of approval was in, and Dad had it. The first time Chet saw my dad, he said, "He's tall, he's handsome, and he has all this leather on. I've done found me a star!"

Chet basically created what became known as the Nashville Sound. Country music had been losing record sales to rock 'n' roll, and Chet and other producers countered by changing country music so it would be more attractive to pop audiences. Fiddles and steel guitars were out, string sections and vocals were in.

Dad had all the respect in the world for Chet and did as he was told, but the Nashville Sound just didn't work for Dad. To

Dad, it was a formula. You could plug in any singer with the right song into that formula and most likely make a hit. But Dad didn't fit into that formula, because he'd always incorporated more of the rock background that he'd picked up from Buddy Holly. The formula musicians took the sound they produced in the recording studio and tried to reproduce it on stage. Dad was the opposite—he produced a sound onstage then reproduced it in the studio.

Chet held on to his belief that he had something special in Dad and encouraged him to keep plugging into that formula. Dad had confidence that if anyone could make it work, Chet was that one. But Dad gradually began to realize that the Nashville Sound was never going to produce a hit for him.

Dad and Chet would record at night, and the producers would work on the recording the next morning. Dad would go back into the studio and discover that someone had added strings and horns, making his songs totally different from what he had recorded the night before.

Chet retired from producing during the 1970s, because he was devoting more time to his responsibilities in leading the label. Chet said stress would kill a person, so he decided to focus on the label. Dad's respect for Chet never diminished. They remained great friends until the day Chet died in 2001, and Dad made sure he was at Chet's funeral.

When Chet stepped out of producing, a roundtable of producers selected by the record label began working with Dad, and he didn't have any respect for their abilities. There was more than one occasion when my dad pulled a gun on a producer and told the producer he wasn't going to change anything about Dad's music.

Dad grew increasingly frustrated. RCA claimed Dad owed the company $200,000. And what was already a tough time got tougher when Dad came down with hepatitis A around the summer of 1972, apparently from some place he had eaten.

During his hospital stay, Dad began reflecting. He was broke and asking for $300,000 to renew his contract. The label wanted to give him a $150,000 advance against royalties. Dad was tired from being on the road so much. He was having kind of a pity party, honestly, when he decided, *Screw it, I'll quit.*

Then Richie Albright came in to talk to Dad. Richie had quit as Dad's drummer because he was tired from all the dates he had been playing and because of his ongoing disagreement with my dad about pot. Dad didn't like pot because it came in large packages and smelled. Cocaine, on the other hand, came in small packages and couldn't be detected by scent. Richie, though, kept doing pot against Dad's wishes, and he'd finally split to work for the rock band Goose Creek Symphony.

When Richie heard my dad was in the hospital and thinking about quitting music, he went to visit Dad and told him not to give up. He pushed Dad to give it one more shot and told him there was a new way of doing music that was called rock 'n' roll. He meant that other rock artists had done something new by taking control of their own music.

Dad didn't understand what Richie was implying.

Richie told Dad that after his contract expired, he wouldn't have anyone telling him what to do and they could make their own music.

Fortunately for Dad, Richie knew a New York music manager named Neil Reshen who could help make this transition.

"Mad Dog on a Leash"

In hindsight, Neil Reshen was the best thing that ever happened to my dad's career.

Neil was a Jewish guy from New York who had studied accounting in college. He started off handling income taxes for musicians and music executives before becoming a manager.

Dad had never had a true manager, because he couldn't afford one. Plus, the record label had convinced him he didn't need one. He had road managers, and Lucky Moeller had been his booking agent, but before Neil, Dad had never had anyone who oversaw the business side of being Waylon Jennings.

Dad called Neil "a mad dog on a leash." He and Neil didn't see each other a lot, because Neil was in New York. But if a matter was important enough, they'd arrange to meet face-to-face. If business called for it, Dad would unleash his mad dog and turn him loose. Neil actually was a sweetheart of a guy as long as you didn't make him mad. But if you did, he could rip you a new one.

Neil had a master plan: Find two artists/bands who were on separate labels and also appeared on other artists' recordings on different labels. Dad and Willie Nelson fit that description, and he convinced Dad and then Willie to let him become their managers.

That gave Neil the right to audit not only RCA (Dad's label) and Columbia (Willie's label) but also the other labels for which they had performed duets to make sure they had been paid correctly. Neil gained access to basically the entire industry. When Neil audited RCA, he discovered that not only did Dad *not* owe RCA $200,000, but RCA owed him $200,000 and had not complied with a renewal clause in his contract. That discovery gave Neil bargaining leverage for renegotiating Dad's contract.

Dad's new contract with RCA rocked the boat big-time, because Neil negotiated for Dad to have complete control of producing his albums. As far as Dad was concerned, he was going to go into the studio and cut the songs he wanted the way he wanted them and deliver them to the label. He was going to give RCA a product to sell, and if it chose not to release his albums, that was on RCA. Dad would have fulfilled his contract and would make his money.

My dad's first album under his new contract was *Honky Tonk Heroes*. Other than Donnie Fritts's and Troy Seals's "We Had It All," every song was written or cowritten by Billy Joe Shaver, a talented young man from Central Texas whom Dad had encouraged to make a go of it in Nashville.

Dad cut that album without big orchestrations or productions; he relied solely on guitars, vocals, and drums. When he delivered the album, RCA didn't want to release *Honky Tonk Heroes* because it sounded "rough" and "not polished enough."

"My contract says I have to turn this in to you," Dad told them. "This is what you've got. Release it or not."

RCA wound up releasing the album in May 1973, and it went Gold. Today, that album is looked to as one of the foundation-laying albums of the Outlaw movement.

Ken Mansfield joined Dad on *Honky Tonk Heroes*, producing the album's only single, "We Had It All." Three years later, he also produced the *Are You Ready for the Country* album that reached number one three times in 1977 and included "Can't You See" and the gospel standard "Precious Memories." Ken also produced songs on other albums of Dad's such as *The Ramblin' Man* (which included the number one hit "Amanda"), *I've Always Been Crazy*, and *Waylon and Willie*. Not only did Ken produce songs with Dad, but Dad also joined him in coproducing four albums with Jessi, including her number one single "I'm Not Lisa." Two of those albums made it to number one.

I never felt Ken received the credit he deserves for *Honky Tonk Heroes* and for his involvement in Dad's career.

A successful music industry executive and record producer, he always seemed very humble, especially considering that the mind-blowing list of people he worked with included the Beach Boys, Glen Campbell, Lou Rawls, Bobbi Gentry, James Taylor, Badfinger, and an English group called the Beatles. It was the Beatles who placed him in charge of Apple Records' American division.

Dad believed Ken understood him better than anyone in the Nashville System. He told *Los Angeles Times* reporter Bob Hilburn in 1976 that Ken was the only producer he truly trusted in the studio. He later made a similar comment to reporter Bob Kirsch for an article published in *Billboard* magazine.

Ken's son, Kevin, was the one who was with me when the garage roof fell in on my yellow Dodge Challenger. I was about sixteen, and Kevin was about fifteen. Our dads considered it good for us to spend time together, so they offered to back any business we wanted to start and run. We decided to open a go-kart track, but that didn't work out because of sound ordinances in Nashville and other location problems.

Kevin and I hung out a lot and had fun running around town in Dad's Cadillac, which was orange with a silver, naked lady on the front with her hair flowing in the wind. The interior was orange-and-white plaid, including an orange-and-white steering wheel cover. We called the car the pimp mobile.

We once took a family vacation to Arizona with the Mansfields, with Dad, Jessi, Jennifer, Buddy, Ken and his wife, and Kevin's sister, Lisa, all piling into Dad's bus. Julie, Kevin, and I followed the bus in the pimp mobile. The three of us loaded up about two hundred joints for the trip and smoked pot all the way to Arizona, although we were smart enough to stay far enough behind the bus so they couldn't see us smoking.

We stopped in Littlefield on the way. The cool thing to do in Littlefield was known as Dragging Main, where the teenagers would cruise up and down the main drag in town. I dragged main in Dad's Caddy!

Ken Mansfield was partly responsible for what I believe was the best band Dad had at any point in his career. Dad already had Ralph Mooney on steel, Richie Albright on drums, Rance Wasson on acoustic rhythm, and Gordon Payne on electric rhythm. When Dad went out to Los Angeles in early 1976 to record *Are You Ready for the Country*, Ken brought in Sherman Hayes to play bass and the husband-and-wife duo of Barny and Carter Robertson as, respectively, piano player and backup singer. Barny and Carter had been doing their own Captain and Tennille–type thing. For Barny on stage, we had a small grand piano, a Wurlitzer organ, and an electric keyboard, and he could play all three in all different directions. Carter was a great backup singer, and at this time, Ken was in the final stages of producing her solo album, called *Shoot the Moon*, for ABC Records.

Dad had that particular band for two or three years until Sherman found religion and moved to a commune in Washington. When Sherman left, they came to me looking for a replacement. I was twenty-one and had no idea why I was the one given that task, other than I hung out with a lot of musicians and perhaps they thought I could easily come up with a replacement. I did find a guy, but he sucked and made it about thirty days before Dad replaced him with Jerry Bridges.

Dad gave Jerry the nickname Jigger because he reminded Dad of my mom's uncle Jigger. Soon after Jigger joined us, we were partying at our hotel and I asked him, "Aren't you a little nervous about being Dad's bass player?"

"Why should I be?" he said.

I began running through the list of Dad's bass players. The first had quit because he didn't want to move to Nashville. The second got shot in a gunfight in Canada. The third owed money to drug dealers and had his fingers cut off. Sherman had broken both of his wrists when he fell while trying to hang a sign in a tree and then moved into a commune. The most recent had barely lasted a month.

"Dad hasn't had a lot of luck with bass players," I summarized.

"No," Jigger softly said.

The next morning I learned that Jigger had suffered a heart attack after I'd left the party. I told the crew about our conversation.

"That might have done it," they told me.

"I didn't mean to give him a heart attack," I said.

Jigger's heart attack caused shuffling of the lineup for that night. Until Jigger showed up out of the blue, ready to play. He had awakened in the hospital that morning and been told about the heart attack and that he would be held until the next day for monitoring. As soon as he had the chance, Jigger unplugged everything attached to him and walked out of the hospital. He still had the stoppers on when he got to the show. He played like nothing had happened and everything was fine. We stuck the stoppers all over his amps as a reminder.

Jamaica with the Cashes

Our family took a trip to Jamaica with Cash's family during some time off in '75. The Cashes had a place there called Cinnamon Hill that looked down on the main road into and out of Montego Bay.

Cinnamon Hill Estates was an old plantation. Behind the main house was a smaller house that had once served as slave quarters. Buddy and I stayed there.

Before we left on our trip, Dad gave us strict instructions not to even think about smoking pot. Rosey, June's daughter, either hadn't received those same orders from her stepdad or chose to ignore them. Rosey had pot with her—good pot, too—and the two of us would sneak off at night and smoke some joints.

Rosey returned home before the rest of us, but she left her pot with me. So then Julie and I started sneaking out to smoke. We didn't finish off what Rosey had given us and, of course, we couldn't leave free pot behind. We took the biggest bud, wrapped it in a baggie, and placed a rubber band around it. We put the baggie in Julie's face cream, covered it up, and put it in her bag. When we arrived back home, Julie opened that bag, and the baggie had shifted during the flight. The baggie with the pot in it was sitting there in plain view.

Cash had taken up photography as a hobby, and while we were in Jamaica, he asked Dad if he could take photos of our family as well as individual photos of each of us. Being young, naturally, a photo shoot wasn't in our vacation plans. But Dad made us pose for Cash, and I'm glad he did. Cash developed the photos after he returned to Nashville, signed his name real small in the bottom right corner like a professional photographer, had the photos professionally framed, and gave each of us the individual shots he took of us and his favorite photo of our family. I am so glad now to have those photos from Cash.

Falling Out with Tompall

Hazel Smith created the *Outlaw* label. Hazel, a country music journalist, was publicist and office manager at Tompall Glaser's Hillbilly Central. She was a marketing genius, and she belongs in the Country Music Hall of Fame, because she promoted the careers of a lot of men and women who are in the Hall. Dad embraced being called an Outlaw—especially because Hazel had deemed him one. Originally, *Outlaw* simply referred to someone who was bucking the Nashville System from within.

Dad had earned the right to play his music the way he wanted to play it. He found a place to record that music at Hillbilly Central, a two-story stucco office building and recording studio that Tompall had bought a couple of blocks from Nashville's Music Row. Dad also set up his office there.

When it came to Nashville, Tompall had an independent streak that stood out like the white running down a skunk's back. That was one reason he and Dad were as close as brothers. Willie Nelson had his song "Me and Paul" about his drummer, Paul English. Dad would sing a version of the song that he called "Me and Tompall."

Dad and Tompall loved to play pinball together. It wasn't like the typical pinball machine most are familiar with. Instead, it was a game in which players tried to line up balls in squares. Depending on how many balls players could get lined up in a row, they could earn free games or even win money.

Dad and Tompall could drops hundreds of dollars in a

pinball session without realizing how much they were spending, one quarter at a time. In fact, the only time I remember Kevin and me getting into trouble together was when we found Dad's stash of quarters for pinball and spent them all. Dad didn't discover what we had done until he went to play pinball and all his quarters were gone.

Dad was very superstitious when it came to pinball. When he inserted a quarter to play, he would hold the back of the quarter so he could place it into the slot without touching the machine. He never directly pushed any buttons, touching them with a butter knife instead. He used a rubber mallet rather than his hands to hit the side of the machine and make the balls go where he wanted. We would often find Dad and Tompall playing pinball at the Burger Boy or Fanny's near their office. After my dad became famous, the Burger Boy owner built a box around the machines to prevent people from bothering Dad while he played.

In Tompall's office, the secretaries, bookkeepers, and office manager sat in the front. Then there was a short hallway, with a conference room on the right and restrooms on the left. At the end of the hall was a doorway without a door. Dad's office was immediately past the doorway and on the right. Tompall's office was farther back, facing the parking lot. The recording studio was upstairs along with a few more offices. When Ken Mansfield came to town, he virtually took over Tompall's office during the day. Some evenings, Ken would migrate upstairs to the studio. Some of those informal sessions found their way onto later albums.

Tompall decided to put a door at the end of that first-floor hall so that he and my dad could have more privacy. Problem was, when the door was left open, half the door blocked the entry into Dad's office, and that hallway door was rarely closed. When Dad would leave his office, he'd smack right into that door. After a handful of such collisions, Dad took the saw blade of a Swiss Army knife, sawed the door in half vertically, and nailed that half outside Tompall's office door with a note attached that read, "See how you like that, you son of a bitch."

Without fanfare, both halves of that door disappeared.

Dad had owned a publishing company called Baron Music to pitch songs, oversee copyrights, and make sure royalty payments were collected and distributed. His brother Tommy ran the company, and Tompall talked Dad into dissolving Baron and bringing it into his publishing company. That cost Tommy his job and a lot of money, and that sparked a big disagreement between my uncle and my dad.

Dad published with Tompall's company and recorded in his studio, including the *Honky Tonk Heroes* and *Wanted! The Outlaws* albums.

Tompall was a musician, too, recording as a solo act and with his brothers, Chuck and Jim, as part of the Glaser Brothers trio. They'd had good success in the late sixties and early seventies, but their careers were beginning to flatten as Dad's was on the way up. Dad included Tompall on the *Outlaws* album cover because he liked Tompall and wanted to help him.

Tompall was part of the Outlaws tour in 1975 with my dad, Jessi, and Willie Nelson. Tompall tried to live up to the Outlaws image—the personal image, not the musical image—and wanted to be different from everyone else on the tour. Instead of traveling in a bus, Tompall came up with the idea of taking a forty-five-foot trailer, making it like the inside of a bus, and traveling behind a semi. Unfortunately for Tompall, he learned that would be against the law.

Jessi, Willie, and Dad were big hits on the tour, but Tompall didn't receive as much love from the audience. Music's a tough business. Like Dad used to tell me, when you're onstage, you have to hold your own. Dad didn't care who opened or closed a show; he just wanted to do his thing well and turn the stage over to whoever was next. But Tompall was clearly fourth of four on the fans' lists.

The tour, which lasted two or three months, ended with Tompall feeling like he hadn't been given the same level of respect as Jessi, Willie, and Dad. Then after the tour, Dad and Tompall got into a dispute over publishing matters. They had trusted each other before, but Dad became convinced that Tompall was stealing money from him. Yet Dad didn't want to pursue any kind of legal action. Embezzling lands a person in prison, and there was no way Dad was going to do that to someone who once was his best friend. The money wasn't the big issue anyway; it was what Tompall was doing to Dad.

They lost their friendship, and to my knowledge they never reconciled. In time, the identical thing happened to Dad and Ken over business matters. Neil had also told Dad that Ken was stealing from Jessi's royalty account. That was ironic, because although Jessi was signed to Ken's Hometown Productions, Ken had her contract assigned to Capitol Records. According to Ken, Neil told Ken to his face that he felt Ken had become too important in the Jennings household and that Neil's accusation was strictly a strategic move to get him out of the picture. The accusation was easily disproved, because Capitol paid Jessi and Ken their royalties separately.

Ken said he was dumbfounded by the absurdity of Neil's accusation, because he had never even seen any of Jessi's statements or money. Dad believed Neil and felt betrayed. Ken was deeply hurt by having his honesty questioned. The argument between Dad and Ken at the Sheraton University Hotel late one night became so heated that it damaged their long, close friendship, and they never reconciled.

New Office, New Logo

Dad left Hillbilly Central, formed a new company called Waylon Jennings Ltd., and purchased an office at 1117 Seventeenth Avenue South, in a house that had been transformed into offices. Dad kept his office there most of the rest of his life, and he recorded next door at American Studios.

The studio was owned by the Cartee brothers, Don and Al, of Memphis. Dad started out leasing the studio for recording sessions, but he disliked finding other artists recording there when he was ready to go into the studio, and he wound up leasing the studio on a yearly basis.

The Cartee brothers gave Dad the run of the studio, except for a room upstairs in the far right back corner. The Cartees told us to stay out of that room. Naturally, the first thing we did was pick the lock on the door. The room was filled with guns, like an armory. We never found out what all those guns were there for, because we weren't exactly going to ask and let them know we'd been in the room.

Neil, Dad's manager, had been talking to Dad about the importance of branding, and after Dad moved into his new office he brought in William Conrad, a member of Ken's Hometown Productions team, to design a new logo.

Dad loved Gene Autry movies, and at the end of Autry's movies, there would be an *A* with wings on it. From that, Dad wanted his logo to be a *W* with wings. After some back-and-forth brainstorming between Dad and Conrad, they settled on an eagle with wings stretched to form a capital *W*. Conrad had the eagle's head on top of the middle stem of the *W* facing right. Dad wanted the head flipped to face left, to be looking toward what Dad considered west.

Dad insisted that the logo be colored Hancock orange. Grandpa Jennings had owned a Hancock service station. Hancock stations were painted Hancock orange, and because of the surplus paint Grandpa received, just about anything outside of his house that needed to be painted turned out Hancock orange. Over the years, the color in Dad's logo has evolved to become more reddish, but originally it was Hancock orange because of Grandpa's service station.

By the time the logo was ready to roll out publicly around 1977, Dad was ultrahot. He'd have an album reach the top of the charts and stay there until his next album came out and replaced it.

10

RULES OF THE ROAD

I had it coming.

I'd held some type of job since I was eleven. In Nashville, I decided to put life on cruise control. Big house, plenty of food, a car I could use—why did I need a job?

While Julie and I were living in Texas, Dad and Jessi had hired Maureen Rafferty to work in their house. During the day, Maureen was principal for a school of troubled boys. At night, she worked for Dad and Jessi. The first time I'd met Maureen, I was fifteen and had hitchhiked with Steve Sellers, a friend I'd made in junior high, to Nashville. I'd thumbed my way down to Houston to spend a couple of weeks with Steve, and he suggested we hitchhike up to Mom's.

Mom's place wouldn't have been what he expected. When we were with Dad, we lived well. At Mom's, we were living in the ghetto. My sister did some research years later and discovered that at the time Mom's neighborhood was one of the most dangerous in the country. We didn't know it then, and we ran around like it was just another safe, quiet neighborhood. When I described the differences between living with my mom and my dad, Steve decided he'd rather hitchhike to Nashville.

Dad and Jessi had moved into yet another new home, and when we reached the vicinity of their house, we called and talked to Maureen before she had left for her day job. We described where we were, and she said she would come pick us up. Bud, who was twelve, happened to be home from school sick that day, and he spotted us from the car and pointed us out to Maureen. Steve and I both had long hair, and we were dirty from hitchhiking for three days. Maureen took us to the house and when we got there, she called Dad.

"Your son Terry just showed up," she told him. "If you would like, I'll stay home today and protect the house."

"You can go to work," Dad told her. "The house doesn't need to be protected from Terry."

When I moved to Nashville, I was living the good life. I wasn't working, and I would go outside at night to grill steaks and leave my mess behind for Maureen to clean up.

After about three or four months of living there, I was sleeping on the couch one day when Maureen woke me up. Maureen was about five foot tall. Although she lost a lot of weight later in life, she had to weigh about three hundred pounds then. I was somewhere around ninety to one hundred pounds, soaking wet *and* with rocks in my pockets.

"You need to find a job," Maureen told me. "You eat too much. You need to get a job, or you'll be sleeping in your broken-down car."

I had a problem with Maureen's eating comment, because she

weighed about three times as much as me. I wasn't the one with the eating problem. She was correct, however, about me needing to get a job. I found a gig working the graveyard shift at an Exxon filling station. I took Dad's car in to work, changed the oil, and flushed the radiator. Then I did the same for Jessi's car, then Julie's. When I ran out of family cars to service, I quit the job.

Dad's office at the time was still in Hillbilly Central. I went into the conference room where there was a telephone and spread a newspaper out to go through the classified advertisements. I was making phone calls for job listings when my dad and Richie walked in.

"I'm just making some phone calls," I told them. "I can get out of your way."

"No, you're fine," Dad said. "We'll talk in my office."

Like a scene right out of a cartoon, Dad and Richie turned and began walking away, then backed up in unison, and faced me again.

"What are you doing?" Dad asked.

"Looking for a job."

"Do you think you can do Beak's job?" Dad asked. Beak's real name was John Ulrick; he was one of Dad's roadies.

"He's sick and won't be able to work," Dad said. "It's only a two-week gig."

"If someone shows me how to do it once," I answered, "then I can do it."

Just like that, I'd found a job. A temporary one, but it was a job.

One of our stops was a fair where we set up on a racetrack. Someone asked if anyone knew how to run spotlights. No one did.

"Terry knows all the songs that will be played," someone else chimed in. "I'm sure he can do it."

There were four spotlights, and I didn't know the first thing about how to run them. I knew that at some point Dad was going to play guitar and Ralph Mooney was going to play steel.

I told the spotlight operators, "Put two lights on Moon and two on Waylon, and I'll tell you when to turn them on." I didn't know that from the distance we were set up, all four spotlights needed to be on one person. Somebody obviously important came up there and yanked the headphones off my head and asked, "What the hell do you think you're doing?"

"They told me to do this, so I am," I said.

"You're not doing a very good job," the guy told me.

"I didn't say I could," I shot back.

Removed from spotlight duty, I went to the stage. I was very attentive, making sure everything was going right for Dad. Apparently no one had done that previously, and after a couple of weeks of ensuring everything was working on the stage during Dad's shows, I was offered the roadie job permanently.

When I got hired, Dad sat me down in his office and told me there were three rules of the road:

1. "Find a good bottle of water and stick with it. The biggest problem with going from town to town is drinking different waters out of the tap. You're used to the tap water in your town. You go to another town and it's different, you'll get a stomach bug."

2. "When we stop to eat, order anything you want on the menu. And then order a cheese sandwich. It's hard to

screw up a cheese sandwich. If the food you order isn't good, you'll have the cheese sandwich and won't have to make everyone wait for you to order another meal."

3. "When the other guys are out raping and pillaging, don't get caught holding the horses."

There wasn't any raping or pillaging going on—at least that I knew of—but the third rule confused me. It took about three years for me to understand that Dad was telling me that if the other guys were out doing things, I needed to be out there with them, because the person who stays behind and holds the horses is the one who gets caught and blamed for everything.

My first assignment was to drive the truck with the band gear on board to Dallas, where the lighting gear would be loaded.

Dad handed me an envelope containing fifty white cross pills (amphetamines).

"This should get you to Dallas," he said.

Fifty was a lot, because white crosses were the real-deal speed.

"That'll help," I told him. "But I don't think I'll take them all at once."

Dad went into his office and shut the door. Then Richie walked by and gave me an ounce of pot.

"This'll get you to Dallas," he told me.

"Thanks," I said. "I'm ready for the road now."

I took a few white crosses, rolled a few joints, and headed off for Dallas.

That was the first time my dad gave me drugs. It surprised me when he did, but I understood that he didn't want me falling asleep at the wheel. The number of pills was excessive, though. I gave away more than I took. It was a nice gesture on Dad's part, but I liked Richie's pot better.

I made it to Dallas fine, parked the truck at a friend's house, partied a little bit that night, took the truck to where it needed to be the next morning, and caught a flight back to Nashville to head out on the road with everyone else.

Number One

In the spring of '74, Dad released *This Time*. The title song was one that Dad had written a few years earlier, but Chet hadn't liked it. Richie talked Dad into giving the song another try, and it became Dad's first number one single. *Dreaming My Dreams*, released in 1975, included the number one single "Are You Sure Hank Done It This Way" and was his first album to be certified gold by RIAA.

His next big album, in January 1976, was *Wanted! The Outlaws*. Dad was playing a lot of road dates but had an album to put out per his contract. So he repackaged old recordings of himself, Jessi, Willie, and Tompall.

"Good Hearted Woman" was the first song on the second side. It sounds like a live duet with Willie, but it really wasn't. Dad laid the tracks down and laid his vocals down, Willie did the same with his vocals, and a clap track was used for the "live" audience. I watched Dad struggle for two days trying to figure out how he could call out Willie's name to introduce him during the song and have the audience respond to make it sound live. He couldn't get it to come out right until he placed a microphone in the corner of the drum booth, opened the door, shouted "Willie!" and shut the door. That's what ended up on the "live" recording.

RCA's marketing department gave the album its title and created a wanted poster of the four of them for the cover. The album went platinum—the first country music album out of Nashville to do so.

"Why did that album go platinum?" Dad asked me.

"Because it sold a million copies," I said.

But at the exact same time, Dad starting answering his own question with "There was a band called the Outlaws that came out, and all those stoned-out hippies are going to the record store asking for 'that new *Outlaws* album,' and the store gave them ours. And once you buy them, you can't take them back."

With *Wanted!* setting country music sales records, RCA couldn't argue with Dad anymore over his bucking the Nashville System.

Things were going better on the road, too. "Mad Dog" Reshen's arrival as Dad's manager in 1972 had made life better for all of us who traveled with him. Before, we had ridden together on one bus, with Dad having the estate room. The band and crew slept in bunks and on couches. Gear and merchandise were carried in a van, and everything else went in the bottom of the bus.

Thanks to Neil and to Dad's success, we grew to three buses—one for Dad and Jessi, one for the band, and one for the crew of nine that consisted of three of Dad's full-time employees plus the lighting crew and sound crew, who were subcontractors. We started carrying our own sound and lighting equipment, and with the gear and merchandise, we needed two semis to get from show to show. The Crickets traveled with us for a while, and they preferred a motor home over a bus. They weren't given one, so they got one on their own.

Our hotels also upgraded significantly, to the types of hotels where the room service hamburgers cost more than the steaks in some restaurants. Dad's allergy to the phrase *per diem* cost him money. With the upgrades, Dad told us to go to the hotel restaurant, eat anything we wanted, and sign the bill to our room. Alcohol delivered to our rooms? No problem. Sign it to the room, and he'd take care of it.

I tried to make Dad see how much money he was spending. I suggested he could help budget by putting the band and crew in less-expensive hotels near cheaper restaurants and having us turn in receipts. He rejected my idea, though, because he wanted everyone to enjoy the same perks he received.

"If I go big," he said, "everybody goes big."

The venues got bigger—and nicer—too. We'd been playing clubs with our big band crammed onto smaller bandstands. One of the places that still stands out is the Cotton Club in Lubbock because of the chicken wire in front of the stage. More bizarre than the fact that the chicken wire was there was that performers welcomed the chicken wire. If the Cotton Club crowd didn't like you, they'd throw beer bottles at you. There's nothing like having to play a set while ducking behind chicken wire. But that sure as heck beats having to duck behind each other.

One night at the Cotton Club, a triangle piece of wood came over the back of the stage and knocked a hole in one of Richie's drums. When that chunk of wood landed, Richie took off one direction and I ran the other. I came back to change the head on the drum. Richie swore he'd find the culprit, but I don't think anyone ever identified him.

As Dad's success mounted, we started playing theaters and arenas with forty-foot stages. Dad believed we needed to keep the band compact or he'd lose his sound. I disagreed and told him we needed to spread things out because from the crowd's perspective, it looked stupid seeing all our equipment bunched together with an abundance of empty stage on either side. Dad didn't give a rip about looks, though.

"They came to hear me, not see me," he'd say with a dismissive wave.

The sound started bleeding into other mics, like Dad's mic picking up the drums. The crew members kept bugging me to do something to fix it. A sudden change for Dad was out of the question, so little by little I had the band spread out when we set up for a show.

After about three weeks of gradual change, Dad came to me and said, "Terry, I know what you are doing. You've been spreading that equipment out. If you're that strong headed, fine, set it up the way y'all want and we'll see if it works or not."

So we set up a real mic line and amp line. We set up monitors, which Dad thought were only for vocals.

"No," I told him. "We're working with a real company here, and we can have anything you want."

And Dad loved the changes.

11

FRIED CHICKEN AND HANK JR.

My official title was drum tech, or drum roadie. My job was to take care of and set up the drummer's equipment. For a lot of years, that meant taking care of Richie Albright.

I was told I'd need to tie down Richie's drums or he would come in every night and reset them. I knew better. I could have glued the drums down and Richie still would reset them at every stop. That was one of Richie's quirks: He was going to move his drums around no matter what. I'd mark the floor with Xs, and Richie would always move the drums then put them right back on my marks.

I knew of other drum techs who had to deal with drummers who wanted great, big drum sets with gongs behind them and demanded that every cymbal be polished and spit-shined every night. Richie wasn't like that. He didn't want his cymbals spit-shined, because that changed their tone. One of the worst things for him was getting a new cymbal and having to break it in.

During shows I had to be on standby for just about anything that could go wrong with the drums. Sometimes the foot pedal on the bass drum would slip out of place or break, in which case I'd have to run a new one to Richie. The high hat could pop off, and I'd replace it without missing a beat. Then there was the common task of replacing a broken drum head.

One time, Richie decided to go with rawhide drum heads instead of plastic. Rawhide was affected by temperature and humidity. I'd have everything set at sound check, but then the stage lights would come on and the rawhide heads would heat up and go limp. Our solution: a squirt gun and a hair dryer. If the drum heads got too tight, I'd squirt them with water. If they became loose, I'd hit them with water and then crank up the hair dryer. Thankfully, the rawhide phase only lasted one tour before Richie switched back to plastic heads.

One year we were playing Chicago Fest, and a drummer from a doo-wop band was brought in to set up Richie's drums. The drummer was from Dover, Delaware, and he decided to make them sound exactly as he thought they should. I was asked if I was okay with that, and I said, "Sure," brought out a bottle of Jack Daniel's, and took a seat to watch the guy we began calling "the pro from Dover" work his magic.

Richie came in to check out his drums and started cussing at me, asking what I had done to his drums. I told him about the pro from Dover and introduced the two to each other.

"I don't know who you are, but you need to get the hell

out of here," Richie said and then told me to fix his drums. Everyone laughed but the pro from Dover.

Richie was especially particular about his bass drum. One night I was asleep in a California hotel and Richie called me to his room. Deacon Proudfoot, Dad's bodyguard, was there too, and he and Richie had ordered four fried chicken meals from room service. They were drunk and high.

"What do you want?" I asked, half asleep.

"Hear this," Richie said, and Deacon picked up a piece of chicken and threw it against the wall.

"Did you hear that?" Richie asked.

Deacon threw the chicken against the wall again in case I hadn't.

"That's what I want my bass drum to sound like," Richie told me.

Deacon said, "We'll call it chicken fat slap back."

"Fine," I said. "I'll get some Kentucky Fried Chicken every time we hit town, and I'll strap it to your kick drum. That'll work perfect." Then I walked out and went back to sleep. I never brought in KFC, but I did get Richie's bass drum as close to the chicken fat slap back sound as I could.

My responsibilities extended well beyond drum tech. I reported directly to Dad and Richie, and Dad trusted me to have his back. As a result, basically everything passed through me. If someone were to ask Dad or Richie a logistical question, their typical response would be "What did Terry say?"

Being a drum tech required thinking on my feet when the unexpected occurred. It didn't take me long to learn to expect the unexpected. I paid close attention to all the band members and knew what every one of them wanted. I knew when they were happy. I knew when they needed a beer. I even knew that at the rate rhythm guitar player Rance Wasson drank beer, he would need to take a leak during the show, and I'd slip a five-gallon bucket behind the amp line for him.

Dad actually wasn't too particular about his guitars. He did insist, though, on having Fender Super Slinky strings, and they had to be changed. He had the Scruggs tuner on the E key. He would lock it into E and then there was another nut he would lock into D. That meant instead of having to retune a guitar to switch from E to D for a different song, just like that he was in D. The problem with those tuners was two of them cost $250, and he went through them like hotcakes because they wore out pretty quickly. Another problem was the Fender phase shifters Dad liked. The wiring inside of them wasn't grounded well, and that caused them to develop a buzz. We would have to take them apart, shield the wires, and put them back together to eliminate the buzz.

The Crickets toured with us for a while in the late '70s, which provided me the opportunity to get to know drummer J. I. Allison, who cowrote "Peggy Sue" with Buddy Holly and Norman Petty. I'd heard that J.I. was a prick, but he was laid-back and loved to have fun. One night, in the middle of the Crickets' first song, the bracket that held J.I.'s stool in place exploded, and the stool collapsed out from under J.I. I don't think J.I. missed a beat, though. He kept on playing.

The stool was mine to fix, but I was in shock at what had happened. I had no idea what to do until CoCo Ray, our guitar tech, ran over to me with a pair of vise grips. J.I. stood up—still playing the drums—while I clamped the vise grips where they would hold the seat in place. Even when I bought a new stool for J.I., I continued to use vise grips on the bracket just in case.

My job kept me busy, and sometimes I couldn't fully appreciate all the people I got the chance to meet. For a year or a year and a half, during the early- to midseventies a young Jay Leno opened some shows for Dad with a thirty-minute comedy routine. I had too many responsibilities to mess around with a comedian, so I heard little of his routines. If I had known Leno was going to take over *The Tonight Show*, I would have paid more attention to him.

Leno must have been funny back then, though, because Dad and the audiences liked him. Years later, he remembered what Dad had done for him and invited Dad and Shooter to be on his show from time to time.

Telling on Hank Jr.

I had to snitch on Hank Williams Jr. for making our job more difficult.

Dad really believed in Hank Jr. and wanted to help his career. Dad grew up in West Texas wanting to be Hank Williams. He never got to meet Hank Sr., who died on New Year's

Day, 1953, at the age of twenty-nine. Hank Jr. was three when his dad passed away, and after Dad moved to Nashville and got to know Audrey, Hank Jr.'s mom, she asked Dad to take her son under his wings.

I remember one time, back around 1976 or '77 while we had the Advent projection television, when Hank Jr. was in his late twenties and came over to Dad's house to watch football with us. (No, Hank didn't ask us if we were ready for some football.) Dad and I wanted to watch the Cowboys game, but Hank kept switching back and forth between games because he had bets placed on them.

Hank was a nice guy. Even today, he's still a big kid, really. Dad took Hank on the road to open for him and paid Hank double his going rate to help him out. In the middle of each set, Hank would show the audience that he could play every instrument on the stage. He would go from the mic to the drums, move over to the piano, continue on to the bass, and then go back to the mic, sit on a stool, and skillfully perform his dad's songs to finish the set.

It was impressive. But he caused problems for us because he would push the amps apart to get to the drums and beat the crap out of the drums and mics. We showed a broken mic to Dad and told him that we were having to pay to replace the mics and I also was needing to replace drum heads because of Hank. I asked my dad, "Can you please tell him to go *around* the amps, not poke holes in the drums, and not beat the mics to death?"

Hank complied with Dad's request, and our tour went great.

Putting Fannies in Seats

Wherever Dad played, we packed the place. The crowds were always rowdy, and that was just the way Dad liked them. He liked fans who got into the show, who jumped up and down and sang along. When we moved into the bigger venues around 1974 or '75, we were surprised that many more people showed up. The smaller clubs were able to charge more for tickets, because they had fewer seats and more people wanting tickets. Now, we were getting the same price for tickets but with more people attending.

Some audiences would stay in their seats and then stand up and applaud for other acts. But when my dad came onto the stage, the fans would press in as close to the stage as they could. We never understood how they could breathe, as crammed in together as they were.

Dad thrived on seeing people in the audience having fun. For a musician, if you're not getting feedback from the audience, you're struggling. You want a response from the audience, because when the fans are enjoying themselves, you'll have a good time, too. Dad really knew how to work an audience. Dad would play a real rockin' tune and wear the audience out, then he'd play a ballad and they'd sit down. Then he'd get them up and all excited again with an upbeat tune. It's like he had the audience on a string—stand 'em up, sit 'em down, stand 'em up, sit 'em down.

Rowdy crowds were good in Dad's eyes, but we all watched out to make sure crowds didn't get too rowdy. People were always trying to get up onto the stage, especially women. Dad didn't mind a hug, but some of the women would hug him so tight that his guitar would press against his belt buckle and dig into his belly. That would just about kill him.

I would signal Dad if a crowd was on the verge of going too far. That got me in trouble one night. I'd seen enough crowds that I could recognize a look in a fan's eyes that said, *I'm about to do something I shouldn't*. That night I saw that look from one man right before he started for the stage. Dad was off to the side of his guitar player, Gordon Payne. I moved around to where I could step in front of Gordon and block the guy's path. But still, the guy headed up onstage toward Gordon and then Dad. While the man was taking a step up, I grabbed him below the knees and pushed him back into the audience. I walked off, and security took over from there. Nobody got hurt.

After the show, Dad told me to never do that again. As it turns out, just as I was grabbing the man's legs, Dad had motioned for Gordon to take off his guitar and hit the man. Dad thought the man might kill me. "If you see someone coming up," Dad told me, "just let them come up. You don't try to stop anyone—you could get hurt."

"What if they hurt you?" I asked him.

"I have people protecting me," Dad said. "I won't get hurt."

What the crowds did, and tried to do, didn't change much after Dad's manager, Neil, came aboard and Dad's star grew—there was just more to watch out for because we were playing to much larger crowds. Fortunately, the incident with the man I tackled never repeated itself, but if it had, I know I would have done the same thing again.

12

DRUGS, GUNS, AND GIRLS

We were a rowdy bunch. There were up to forty of us traveling with Dad, including his band and crew, security, and the sound and light crews. Spending as much time on the road as we did, we had to figure out ways to entertain ourselves.

Drugs, guns, and girls became three constants on the road.

Dad had been booked for a show at the California Institution for Women state prison in Chino in 1978 or '79. When our bus pulled up to the gate, a guard told us that in order for the bus to enter, we would have to turn in all our weapons. The driver surrendered two shotguns and two handguns. The rest of the crew started placing their handguns in a pile. Observing the expanding pile, the guard suggested it might be simpler if we just kept the bus outside the fence. I was happy to hear that, because if they had asked if we had any drugs, we would all have been headed to the pen.

We weren't sure what to expect from an all-female crowd. Even the all-female stagehands were prisoners. CoCo, the guitar tech, would carry a near two-foot-long piece of twelve-aught cable that he would use to thump people who were getting a little rowdy. During the show, as Dad played onstage, we noticed that instead of looking at Dad, the audience was looking to his right. Dad looked over there to see CoCo had stuffed that cable down his pants and was stroking it. Dad about busted up laughing right there on the sage.

"CoCo!" he shouted. "Cut that out!"

It wasn't the smartest thing for CoCo to do in front of a large room filled with female prisoners.

Another memorable gig took place in the midseventies at the Omni Coliseum in Atlanta, which was connected to the Omni Hotel. Because other rock bands had torn up their rooms, the hotel had a rule that forbade anyone playing the coliseum from staying there. The first time we got booked at the coliseum, though, they let us stay in the hotel, because they figured a country band was like a gospel group and wouldn't cause any trouble. Boy, were they wrong.

For fun, one of our lighting guys built a small "bomb" out of a butane can and threw it into a grassy area he thought was a park. The grassy area turned out to be on the property of a bank and the explosion made the bank employees think they were being robbed. We were able to clear that up with the police. But the next time we played Atlanta, we couldn't stay in the Omni Hotel.

They say experience is the best teacher. Mr. Experience taught us a valuable lesson on another trip to Atlanta. Richie came up onstage and started playing. When he turned around to where I could get a good look at him, I noticed he was swaying a little bit.

"You all right?" I asked him.

"Go check on Waylon," he told me. "Tell him everything's gonna be okay. It'll be over in a little bit. It's called Atlanta Dog." I walked into the dressing room, and Dad was lying on a table with a bunch of people around him. I told everyone except Deacon to get out.

"We're fixin' to take your dad to the hospital," Deacon said. "There's something wrong with him."

"Richie told me to tell Dad that everything will be okay—that it was Atlanta Dog," I told Deacon.

I asked around later and found out that some guy had offered Dad and Richie a bump of coke. But he gave them Atlanta Dog, which is a bunch of junk with PCP and who knows what else mixed together. When we went onstage, I had to help hold Richie up as he played. He was swinging and missing his drums. Dad was out of tune and slurring his words. We made it through the night, but it was our worst show ever. Dad broke his own rule that night: *Don't take nothing from nobody you don't know and trust. We have plenty of our own stuff here.*

In '78, we played at the opening of the Buddy Holly Center in downtown Lubbock. A big statue of Buddy stood out front. It was a special gig for Dad. The Crickets and Tony Joe White were also there, and it was Tony Joe's first time on the road with us. Dad didn't usually show up for sound checks, but he did that day and then returned to his bus.

After Dad left, someone shouted "Crazy Eight!" That was a game we'd play where we'd take a gram of cocaine—at $100 a gram—and split it eight ways. Eight people would each pay one-eighth of the cost and do a line.

When we heard "Crazy Eight!" we all went to the crew bus. Unfortunately, we didn't check first to make sure at least one of us remained behind to actually do some work. Dad went back inside the Buddy Holly Center while we were playing Crazy Eight and found Tony Joe and his band standing there without a crew. After we'd finished our coke, we waltzed back in ready to work. Dad promptly started cussing each and every one of us.

"You disrespected my friend!" he yelled at us.

"We thought..." was about as far as we got with our explanation before Dad interrupted to tell us he didn't care to hear what we thought.

After Dad finished, we went over to Tony Joe to apologize.

"It's cool, man," he told us. "Waylon's overreacting."

Tony Joe might have been the most laid-back person on the planet. I don't think it was possible to upset Tony Joe. I know that I would have been mad at us. But that's how into drugs we were.

Close Call

I would get cocaine from Dad and pot through the crew network.

From years of touring, the crew built up a network of people across the country who could supply us with pot when we ran out during a tour. Sometimes I'd go to Dad with another crew member, Randy Fletcher, who took care of the amp lines, and say, "It's been a rough one." Dad would dump some coke in a bag and say, "Y'all can split it up."

We wound up in a bad spot, though, at a place in the Midwest where we didn't have a trustworthy supplier. We found a guy who sold us a quarter pound of good pot for a cheap price. I placed the pot in my Halliburton briefcase and took it to the bus.

A few hours later, the police showed up at the show and told us they received notification that a bomb had been placed on the stage. The band cleared the stage. The crew starting helping the police search for the bomb. That probably says something about the collective IQ of the crew. Dad sent word for the crew to get out of there and let the cops handle the search.

The police told us that the bomb threat specifically stated that the bomb was inside a Halliburton briefcase, and they asked everyone to open their briefcases. Every one of us had our briefcases with us except me. Mine, with the pot inside, was still on the bus. The police looked through the briefcases and when they didn't find a bomb—or anything else illegal—they said the bomb scare was over. The band went back to the stage and finished the show.

At that time Dad was using one amp instead of the two amps he used later. We had placed a wedge inside the amp above the speaker and leaned it back so we could nail it into the stage with a two-by-four. After we had gone back onstage following the bomb search, the amp fell in the middle of a song, landing with a thunderous *Boom!* For a moment Dad believed the bomb had been found after all, while I thought we were going to have to peel Dad off the third row. Later, it occurred to us that we had probably been set up, and that our seller was a cop.

In all my years with Dad, I missed one show because of

drugs. It was 1976 or '77, and I'd been awake for seven days straight. Staying up for days at a time like that was part of our lives on the road. That particular time, I told CoCo, "This cocaine ain't working. Nothing is working. Do you have anything that works?"

He handed me a yellow, plastic-looking pill that had "MF" on it. Most don't need two guesses to figure out what we called those pills. We also called them L.A. Turnarounds, because if you took one, you could drive to Los Angeles, turn around, and come all the way back home without sleeping.

Dad used those for years. He'd set a pill on the table beside his bed, set his alarm for early in the morning, wake up to take the pill, and then in about an hour he'd be wide awake.

I took a nap and planned on the pill waking me up in an hour so I'd be ready for the show. Except once I fell asleep, I didn't wake up. They shook me and tried all kinds of things to wake me, but nothing worked. I was breathing, so they left me alone. I didn't wake up until after the show was over and the bus was back at the hotel.

I went to the hotel bar for a drink, and Richie came in and told me to go with him. He took me to my dad's room.

"There's no excuse for missing a show," Dad told me. "The show must go on. If you can't handle your drugs, then you need to get more sleep. So, what is your excuse for missing the show?"

"I guess I missed my mouth," I said.

Dad and Richie laughed.

"Don't miss a show again," Dad told me.

And I didn't.

Fences and Biscuits

When it came to girls, those of us on the crew sat around and caught the ones that bounced off Dad.

One of the first questions I asked when I went on the road with Dad was, "Why on God's green earth are we playing a northern tour in the middle of winter? We should be down south in the winter and up north in the summer."

"Terry, you got that wrong," Dad corrected me. "It's hunting season. All the men are in the woods, and all the girls will be at the bar."

It didn't take long to realize Dad knew what he was talking about.

Dad would keep extra rooms in hotels for girls. There'd be a room for him and Jessi, but he'd spend a lot of his time on the bus or hanging out in the other guys' rooms. We'd be playing cards and Dad would say, "I'll be back." Then he'd go hit a room where one of his girlfriends was waiting. We could always tell what he'd been up to because he'd come back showered. There'd be times on the road when he'd go two, three, four days without showering. Then he'd shower four times in one night. Uh-huh, we knew what that meant.

Dad didn't like pot, but some of the girls he'd visit with did. He'd call me up and ask, "Got any pot?"

This happened enough that I knew where the conversation was headed, but I'd still say, "You don't like pot."

"I know, but this girl up here does." I'd roll up a couple of joints for Dad because he didn't know how to, stick them inside a magazine, and then go to the room, knock on the door, and hand him the magazine.

There were two important phrases to know on the crew: "building fences" and "pass the biscuits." When we were at a show and spotted a lady we liked, we started building a fence around her. The key was to lay it on thick with her so none of the other guys could steal her away. Most of the crew could build pretty big fences. Dad's fences, however, were made of steel and fifty feet high. We couldn't climb over them, dig under them, or work our way through them. And we couldn't build a fence that could keep Dad out, either. There was no stealing a girl away from Dad and no preventing him from taking ours.

That leads to passing the biscuits.

Say, for example, that I had a lady in my room. Dad might call up and ask, "You through with that girl up there?"

No matter the answer, Dad would say, "Pass the biscuits."

Then I'd have to say to my guest, "Waylon wants to see you down in room so-and-so." Off she'd run and then come back a little later. All of us on the crew would "pass the biscuits" to each other. CoCo and Dad were friends with a stripper for a while. Not only did they know that they were both sleeping with her, they would take a permanent marker and write notes to each other on her belly. Nobody that I knew of ever forced a girl into doing anything she didn't want to do. Dad had built up a stable from running around the country for years. Dad didn't have merely a little black book of phone numbers—he had a *thick* little black book that he carried in his vest pocket. He'd kept that book for so long and used it so often that it had to be held together by rubber bands. He'd have certain girls in certain towns that he'd hook up with when we went through, and they would keep up with our schedule and know when Dad was coming into town. If they didn't show up, it was easy for him to find a backup. Sometimes he would arrange to have girls fly in to where we would be.

And, of course, he could snag anyone's girlfriend anytime he wanted.

We were playing the Cotton Club in Lubbock, and I noticed a really good-looking redhead. I got her seats on the front row and we planned on going to the hotel when my merch sales were done. After I packed up the last T-shirts, she was gone. I looked everywhere for her but couldn't find her. So I went to the bus. There, someone said, "We can't leave yet. Waylon's not ready to leave." We kept waiting until Dad finally came walking out of the back room on the bus with that redhead.

When I say Dad could snag anyone's woman, I do mean anyone's. That wasn't limited to just the band and crew. Once, back when he was married to Barbara, a blonde and her husband were visiting backstage. The man was ready to leave, but his wife wasn't. He'd say, "Let's go home," and she'd tell him, "Not yet. I want to stay here and talk to Waylon."

After one time when the man asked if she was ready to leave and she again said no, Dad pulled the man off to the side and told him, "I used to have a wife just like her. I'd try to get her to leave someplace, and she wouldn't leave. Finally, one time, I told her to find her own ride home and left her. She never did that again."

The man nodded and walked back over to his wife.

"Are you ready to go home?" he asked.

"No," she answered.

"I'm leaving," he told her. "You find your own ride home."

As the man walked away, Dad went over to the blonde and told her, "Let's get out of here before he comes back."

Around late 1975 or early '76, Dad went to Athens, Texas, to have all his teeth removed and replaced with implants. He had some teeth that were getting loose, and with the high-profile Outlaw tour coming up, Dad thought he needed to look flawless.

I drove down to Athens with my girlfriend and checked on Dad, who was recuperating in his hotel room. He smiled, and his gums looked all beaten up because they'd had to rough them up so they would grow over the implants. Look at a picture of Dad's smile beginning with that tour, and it's clear that the implants came out fine. But that was a rough procedure.

In the same hotel, there were some tourists from the Middle East. They wanted cowboy hats, and Jessi suggested I take them to a Western store and help them pick out good cowboy hats. While I was helping them shop, out of the corner of my eye I spotted a lady come out of the dressing room. I caught enough of a glimpse to recognize her as one of Dad's girlfriends. She jumped back into the dressing room and stayed inside for a long time. When she did finally come back out, I asked what she was doing. She told me I couldn't tell anyone she was there.

Even while he was in the middle of having all his teeth removed, Dad had summoned a girlfriend down to East Texas.

Groupies

Dad used to say that rock stars had groupies, but country stars had snuff queens. That was a joke. I think the most common perception of groupies was that they were trashy or desperate. That wasn't the case at all. We had high-society women and actresses asking crew members—who served as the gatekeepers—to allow them backstage. If they looked good, they received a pass.

We also had underage girls trying to get with us, but we were very careful to make sure they didn't ever make it backstage. We knew the trouble that could cause. We carried guns and we were doing drugs and our morals may have been shaky, but none of us was about to do anything illegal with women. They had to be of age and they had to give full consent.

Now that doesn't mean we didn't try hard sometimes to win that consent. One incident that stands out was while we were playing, of all places, at Oral Roberts University in Tulsa, Oklahoma. She was eighteen and drop-dead gorgeous. A member of the lighting crew named Hardy tried and tried and tried to get her to go with him, but she wouldn't. Dad even made his pitch and failed. "Somebody needs to go screw that girl," Dad finally told us, "or somebody needs to send her home."

The girl left, but Hardy had fallen in love with her. The truck was backed up with the ramp pulled out. I'd been walking up and down that ramp all day. Hardy got off the bus and walked up the ramp into the back of the truck. He came back to the edge of the ramp, looked around, and asked, "Where's that g——d—— girl at?" The instant those words left his mouth, the ramp flipped up and Hardy fell and broke his leg. I guess you don't say what Hardy said at Oral Roberts University.

I saw the same girl some years later in Lubbock. I'm bad with names, but I don't forget faces. One of the crew came to me and said, "So-and-so wants to talk to you."

"Who's she?" I asked.

"Some pretty girl back here," he said, pointing, and I recognized her face right away.

I went over to talk with her. She had married some rich guy and had big diamonds on her fingers. Her husband wasn't with her, though, so I gave it a shot. She turned me down again.

Dad couldn't get out in public much. But there's one story about him venturing out among the people that still makes me laugh. We were playing in Miami in 1983 and staying on the beach. I was outside the hotel drinking at the Tiki Bar. I was so bad then that I'd stuffed a bottle of Jack Daniel's in a bush just in case I couldn't find what I wanted at the bar. There were people all up and down the beach, and there were a bunch of girls running around topless. I got pretty drunk at the bar and needed a bump, so I went up to Dad's room to see if I could get one from him.

"Sure," he said. "What are y'all doing?"

"We're down there checking out them naked girls," I told him.

"What naked girls?"

I took him over to the window.

"See that little Tiki Bar there, that hut?" I asked him.

"Yeah."

"Go over three rows and up two."

"I'll be damned!" Dad exclaimed. "She's naked, ain't she?"

I left Dad's room to go back down to enjoy the scenery. I was sitting at the bar with fellow crew member Randy Fletcher, whom we called "Baja Bob."

He punched me in the arm and said, "Look at this."

I turned around to see Dad walking toward the women in full Waylon gear: vest, hat, boots, and jeans. That was one time when he didn't mind being recognized in public.

The closest we ever came to getting into any trouble over women was in 1979 when we played near Columbia University. CoCo and I had a couple of college-aged girls on the bus and we were ready to leave.

"Bus started. Time to get off," I told them.

They didn't say anything.

"Bus is moving. Get off or you're going to Arizona."

Still nothing.

"We're at the last stop sign before we leave town. This is your last chance."

The two girls made the trip to Arizona with us.

Two or three days later, Marylou Hyatt, Dad's office manager, called me. "Did y'all take two girls from Columbia University?" she asked me.

"We've got two girls with us," I said. "I don't know if they're from Columbia University or not."

"The school's dean wants them back," Marylou told me. "Do you think you can get them back to their school?"

We bought two plane tickets and sent them home.

The Good Life

On our tours, the most time I got to spend with my dad was after shows. By being on the road with him, I was able to see more of that side of him than I would have at home.

As part of the crew, I would be busy getting everything ready for the shows, but after we were done at night, we could spend time together. On off days, I'd hang out with Dad on his bus, and sometimes I'd ride with him to the next stop. But most of the time I'd travel on the crew bus, because we had to be the first ones there to start setting up.

To pass the time on the road, we played a lot of cards. Dad loved having me as his Spades partner. We had been paired so many times that after our first play, we knew what was in the other's hand. We also played Farkle, a dice game that some called Rat's Ass. We always played for money, and Dad was the chip holder. The chips were worth ten times their amount. A one-dollar chip was worth ten dollars, on up to a $100 chip that was worth a thousand bucks. I still have a five-dollar chip at my house. My dad owes me fifty bucks, and I plan on collecting from him.

There were plenty of pranks, too, with Dad chief among the pranksters. Dad liked to go into a band or crew member's bathroom with a tube of Super Glue and glue toothbrushes,

hairbrushes, deodorant, cologne—anything movable, really—
to the counter. One time, he glued the handset of a phone to
the square base and when his road manager, David Trask,
answered the phone, he picked up the glued handset so fast
that the entire base came with it and struck David in the side
of the head, almost knocking him out.

Those were great times. To paraphrase Jimmy Buffett, some
of it was magic, some of it was tragic, but it was a good life
all the way.

Wrong Kind of Outlaw

Dad had named his T-shirt company Outlaw Enterprises. He
came to regret that, thanks to me. After my first tour on the
road in 1972, when we had been gone for six months, I came
back home and had a lot of fun. There were six months of
paychecks with my name on them when I returned. I didn't
know I would be receiving checks; I thought my pay was having my expenses covered and the spending money I was given
while out on the road.

I cashed my checks and went out and picked up a nice, blue
jean jacket with fancy blue jeans, a nice shirt, and a pair of
expensive boots. I put on my new clothes and borrowed Julie's
car for a night on the town.

Julie gave me two joints that I placed in my jacket pocket.
I burned one in the car and put the roach in the ashtray. Pre-
dictably for my luck, a couple of policemen pulled me over. I
had no idea what I had done wrong and inquired as to what

my transgression could be. One of the cops told me I was driving—and I'm not making this up—"too correctly."

"Anybody who drives as correctly as you were," he told me, "draws suspicion."

One of the cops searched me and reached into my jacket pocket. I was busted.

The cops debated whether they should take me in, and another cop showed up and sided with the one who wanted to take me in. They took the roach from the ashtray and escorted me to the backseat of their police car. From jail, I called Dad, who came to pick me up. When I was going through the paperwork to be released, I was asked the name of my employer.

"Outlaw Enterprises," I answered.

Dad elbowed me in the side.

"That's true," I told him.

"Well," he said, "we'll have to change that name."

Dad gave the one cop who had wanted to let me go at the scene an acoustic guitar from his backseat. That gesture wound up paying dividends for me later when I bought a Formula 400 Trans Am. There was a traffic light at the end of Sixteenth Avenue on Nashville's Music Row. If I was the first in line stopped at the light, I'd punch the gas when the light turned green. Most of the time, rookie cops patrolled that area, and they would pull me over. The cop to whom Dad had given the guitar trained most of them, and he'd always tell the rookie, "I'll take care of this one."

"Terry," he'd say to me, "you're gonna have to quit doing that. We're gonna have to write you up one of these days. And air that car out—it smells like pot."

13

ON THE ROAD
WITH WILLIE

Dad's friendship with Willie Nelson dated all the way back to their first meeting, when Dad was moving from Arizona to Nashville. In addition to their Texas roots—Willie was born in the small, Central Texas town of Abbott—Dad's and Willie's debut albums were released in the same period, and they held a mutual respect for each other's music.

Dad and Willie were different sides of the same coin. They were like brothers in that one of them could call the other one a son of a bitch, but if someone else said the same thing about one of them, Dad or Willie would jump to the other's defense, which would be expressed in rather colorful language. Dad and Willie would get along great, and then one of them would piss the other off and they'd quit talking for a little while. Then they'd put it behind them and move on like nothing had happened. Every time.

Dad made Willie Nelson's Fourth of July Picnic an annual part of his tours. Willie's event originated with the Dripping Springs Reunion in 1972 at the Hurlbut Ranch in Dripping Springs, Texas. That event included Dad, Willie, Kris Kristofferson, Tex Ritter, Tom T. Hall, Hank Snow, Earl Scruggs, Roy Acuff, and Sonny James. Big names, but it was run like a small-time event. I describe the Reunion as a six-pack of beer, a bag of hot dogs and buns, and two portable toilets. Neon lights were used for lighting, and when you turn on a neon light in Texas, every bug within a hundred miles flocks to it. Dad was inhaling bugs onstage and coughing. The event was barely promoted because of a lack of money. Only twenty thousand people showed up, but Willie knew he was on to something, and that led to his first Fourth of July Picnic in 1973.

To put the picnic together, Willie trusted people he shouldn't have. Money disappeared and acts didn't get paid. Dad didn't receive a cent the first three years he was there. In fact, Dad would take money out of the safe on his bus to pay acts for Willie. Another year, there were supposedly eighty thousand tickets sold. When I went to collect Dad's money from the organizers, they told me that only twenty thousand of those tickets were actually purchased and the rest were bootlegged. I wasn't buying that, and I told them that if Waylon didn't get paid, he'd pack up and leave. Lo and behold, the money mysteriously appeared. That was the first year Dad got paid for doing the Picnic, although I still wonder if he received the correct amount.

Over time Willie's people perfected the picnic and began

moving it around to different places mostly in Texas, but those early years were pretty touch and go. Dad was going to take part no matter what, though, because he and Willie were tight, and Dad would do anything he could to help a good friend.

Dad and Willie first started touring together regularly in 1975, during the *Outlaw* album phase. In 1976, they were the two biggest names on the release of the *Wanted! The Outlaws* album, and they won the Country Music Association's Vocal Duo of the Year and Single of the Year for "Good Hearted Woman." *Wanted! The Outlaws* also was named Album of the Year.

Despite their nominations, both had agreed to boycott the CMA awards that year. Dad wasn't a member of the CMA, and he didn't like the block voting that determined the winners back in those days. Only CMA members could vote, and all the major record labels and other large music industry organizations, such as publishing companies and management companies, would sign up their employees as CMA members and make deals to manipulate the vote.

Dad had attended the awards show in '75, when he was up for Vocalist of the Year and Male Entertainer of the Year. But the only reason he went was because Jessi had been nominated for Song of the Year for "I'm Not Lisa" and for Female Vocalist of the Year. The only win between the two of them that night was Dad for Male Vocalist. That's the year that John Denver won Entertainer of the Year and Charlie Rich burned the piece of paper with Denver's name on it as soon as he had announced that Denver had won. As if singing "Thank God

Dad as a 15-year-old high school freshman. He was kicked out of music class for "lack of ability." Less than two years later, he met my mom, Maxine Lawrence.

Dad's first 15 minutes of fame as a local DJ at KVOW in Littlefield, Texas, in 1955.

Dad and Mom showing off their firstborn, me, at Grandma Bill and Gabby's house, 1957.

Promo shot from Dad's biggest DJ job at KLLL radio station in Lubbock, Texas. To quote Mark Knopfler, "Waylon is the only person I know who can say I was sitting there talking to Buddy Holly, Elvis Presley, and Roy Orbison and not be lying."

Dad with me and baby Julie at home in Levelland, Texas. Dad's probably thinking, "Watching these kids makes me thirsty, and I've got to meet Buddy Holly in New York in a couple of weeks knowing how to play bass guitar."

Family photo from 1965 in Scottsdale, Arizona. A second house divided. Back row: Dad; his second wife, Lynne; Julie; and me. Front row: Tomi Lynne and Buddy.

Me, Dad, Jesse, and Jennifer at Dad's surprise birthday party aboard the *Belle Carol* riverboat. After all the meeting and greeting, Dad blew out the candles on his cake. When the *Belle Carol* was ready to leave the dock, Dad jumped off the boat and left us on a two-hour cruise. *Photo courtesy Audrey Winters.*

Don Zimmerman, president of Capitol Records; Ken Mansfield, Jessi's producer; Jessi Colter; Al Coury, A&R director of Capitol Records; and Dad at Ken Mansfield's Laurel Canyon estate, the legendary "Hangover House," in 1975 celebrating "I'm Not Lisa" landing at #1 on the Billboard chart. *Photo courtesy Ken Mansfield.*

Ken Mansfield, Rick Cunha, Dad, and Ken's son Kevin Mansfield at Tompall's Hillbilly Hotel studio in Nashville where Ken was producing Rick Cunha's *Moving Pictures* album for CBS Records. Dad dropped in to give Ken a hand mixing Rick's record. That was the Outlaw way we made records. *Photo courtesy Kevin Mansfield.*

The Jennings and Cash families spend Thanksgiving together in Jamaica. Cash's new hobby was photography, and he had asked Dad if we would all allow him to take some photos of the family and us individually. Buddy, Jennifer, Jessi, Dad, Julie, and me. *Photo by Johnny Cash, courtesy Terry Jennings Private Collection.*

Cash took this photo of me and gave it to me as a thank-you gift for doing the photo shoot with him. Cash's Cinnamon Hill estate in Jamaica, 1975. *Photo by Johnny Cash, courtesy Terry Jennings Private Collection.*

Me, Jessi, Shooter, and the 39th president in the Oval Office. Nashville hillbillies meet D.C. hillbillies, 1980. Jimmy Carter autographed this photo and mailed it to me.

Hank Williams, Jr., joins Dad for "Are You Sure Hank Done It This Way" on Halloween 1980 in Oakland, California. *Photo credit: C .V. Gouveia.*

Dad getting rowdy during his set on July 25, 1983, in San Jose, California, among thousands of fans and hundreds of Hell's Angels. *Photo credit: C .V. Gouveia.*

Willie joins Dad's set in San Jose, California, for "Good Hearted Woman." *Photo credit: C .V. Gouveia.*

Deana, Buddy, me, and Julie backstage at Billy Bob's Texas in 1983 chilling before the show starts. *Photo by Jerry Floyd, courtesy Terry Jennings Private Collection.*

Me, Cash, Dad, and Jessi at a sobriety party for Dad at Cash's house in Tennessee. I'm introducing myself to Dad, as if we had never met before. I thought it would be funny, but Dad didn't see the humor.

Johnny Cash and Dad on the set of *Stagecoach*. Don't them Outlaws look slick with guns and slickers? *Photo credit: Kal Roberts courtesy of Lightstorm Photography.*

Me, Debra, Jessi, and Dad at Southern Comfort—Dad and Jessi's home in Brentwood, Tennessee. Less than a year later, Debra and I would enter into a three-fold marriage.

Dad's mom making sure Willie plays dominoes right at the Waylon Jennings Day Celebration. Grandma played Willie next and won.

My second-born son, Johnny, with Dad on his bus on July 4, 1991. Dad is wearing a baseball cap because Johnny took his sombrero.

Dad, Josh, Jessi, Debra, Shooter, and me in 1991, enjoying family time before being seated for a meal out on the town in Nashville. *Photo courtesy Kermit Heimann.*

Josh, Dad, me, and Grandma Jennings. Four generations of Jenningses at the Littlefield Center, 1992, for the Jennings Reunion and Waylon Jennings Day Celebration. *Photo courtesy Kermit Heimann.*

My oldest son, Whey Jennings, with Dad at the Opryland Hotel in Nashville, waiting for the Christmas laser light show in December 1994.

Me and Dad on the back patio at Southern Comfort discussing his retirement. It took a while to convince him it was the right thing to do.

I'm a Country Boy" had made Denver an elite country singer. (Olivia Newton-John had won the Female Vocalist award the year before that.)

So Dad wasn't in the mood for another CMA appearance in '76 despite being nominated for five awards, including Entertainer of the Year again. He and Willie agreed on their boycott even though it was the first year two men had been nominated for the Vocal Duo award. Before, all the nominees had been a male-female duo. There were a lot of jokes around Nashville about which one—Dad or Willie—was the woman between them, and that it must have been Willie because he had the long hair.

Dad and I were watching the awards on TV at Dad's house, and when he and Willie were announced as winners of the Vocal Duo of the Year award, lo and behold, there was Willie on the TV, strolling onto the stage to accept the award. Willie said, "On behalf of me and Ol' Waylon, we would like to" blah, blah, blah.

Well, that pissed Dad off even more than he already was about the CMAs.

"That redheaded son of a bitch!" he shouted at the TV. The show continued with Willie strutting out there onstage and saying, "On behalf of me and Ol' Waylon, we would like to accept the award for Single of the Year," and then "On behalf of me and Ol' Waylon, we would like to accept the award for Album of the Year." Dad was beside himself. He had submitted *Wanted!* as his album concept to his own record label via his contract. He'd invited Willie to be a part of the album along with Jessi and Tompall.

Dad did get a laugh, however, when the Statler Brothers went onstage after being announced as Vocal Group of the Year and started their acceptance speech by saying, "On behalf of us and Ol' Waylon, we would like to accept…" But that didn't make Dad any less pissed off at Willie.

We still had tours scheduled with Willie, and I was worried about what Dad might do to get back at Willie. He grunted and cussed Willie and remained mad at him for a while, but the tour dates went on as scheduled and, just like every other time one of them got upset at the other, they got over it. That's not to say, however, that Dad ever let Willie forget about that night.

Little Willie and Little Waylon

Willie had three children from his first marriage: Lana, Susie, and William Jr., who went by Billy. When I was nineteen, Billy and I were introduced to each other in Tulsa by Willie's stage manager, Poodie Locke, who said, "Little Willie, meet Little Waylon." The way to greet someone in those days was to say, "You want a bump?" We went to my room, and it quickly became a game of each trying to one-up the other. Billy poured out one gram of cocaine, and we snorted it. I poured out about two grams, and we snorted that, also. We were gagging all the way down the stairs. Billy and I became good friends.

Later, in Nashville, we had been out drinking together and I was driving back to a hotel. I was late seeing an exit, swerved the car, and we hit a median. All four tires blew out and my car got stuck on the median. We decided to walk to our destination. Billy saw a silver can opener, grabbed it, and stuck it in his back pocket.

We both had to take a leak, so we did. Just my luck, a couple of cops came by. Billy had his thumbs in his back pocket, and one of the officers asked what we were doing. We apologized, saying we had to go and couldn't wait.

The cop informed us that we could be arrested for public lewdness. Billy shifted around, and the silver of the can opener flashed where the cops could see it. They drew their guns and asked Billy what was in his pocket.

"A can opener," he told them.

They told us not to move, came over to Billy, and eased the can opener out of his back pocket. The cops were mad at us by that point and took us to jail. We were to be arraigned that night for public drunkenness. Billy told me that he knew the judge and that I should let him do all the talking. I told him I could speak for myself, thank you. Billy said he could get us out of our mess and then said the two words which should have served as a red flag: "Trust me."

We appeared before the judge, and he asked how we wanted to plead.

Billy spoke up: "We plead 'F—— you,' Judge."

"Billy!" I said.

Too late. The judge threw us in jail, and Willie's people had to bail us out. On top of that, my car had been impounded, and it took me a week to get it back.

Willie's Valet

In 1977, Willie sang a guest vocal on "Luckenbach, Texas (Back to the Basics of Love)," which was one of Dad's biggest hit singles. The next January, they released an album together, and *Waylon and Willie* spent more than two months at number one on the country album charts. With their chart-topping collaborations, it made sense for Dad and Willie to tour together. My favorite memory of the Dad and Willie tours was when I would get my buzz on and be on the stage while Willie performed his *Red Headed Stranger* album from one end to the other. I still get goose bumps thinking about that.

Columbia hadn't wanted to release *Red Headed Stranger*, because it was a concept album and they thought there were only a couple of singles on the album, in "Blue Eyes Crying in the Rain" and "Remember Me." Dad liked Willie's album and went to New York City to visit Columbia's producers on Willie's behalf. Columbia released the album, it went double platinum, and many say it is Willie's greatest album ever.

Willie had come down hard against cocaine and speed on the tours. "You're wired, you're fired" was his rule. Dad, meanwhile, didn't like drinking and pot, and he'd fire you if you were too drunk or high on pot to do your job. My dad was always on my butt about carrying around a bottle of Jack Daniel's and my eyes being red all the time. He even told me, "I would like to see you one time without them damn red eyes from smoking pot."

The first bus Dad had bought evolved into the crew bus. Neither Willie nor Dad would get on that bus.

Knowing that neither of our bosses would be on the crew bus, the two crews would get onto that bus and do whatever we wanted. We named the bus Loopy, because it was the loophole where we could do our drugs of choice. Dad didn't know why we called the bus Loopy—or what took place inside it—until years later when I told him. "You sons of bitches," he told me with a big laugh.

I remember one outdoor show that Dad and Willie played with some other bands, and they were the openers. For Dad's part of the show, the Waylors would do a little set, Jessi would come out and join the Waylors, and then the Crickets would follow. As the Crickets were wrapping up, Dad's band would come out, and they and Dad would join them for a medley of Buddy Holly and Cricket songs. The Crickets would exit, and Dad's set would begin.

During the Waylors and the Crickets sets, fans were throwing beer cans at us. The fans didn't throw beer at Jessi. I guess they were being respectful of the lady. But when she wasn't onstage, they were letting us have it. One can knocked a dent in the drums. Stagehands lined up at the front to try to knock the cans out of the air. I was mad by the time Dad showed up, and I warned him what was happening and to be careful.

"I'll take care of it," he assured me.

So Dad goes onstage and here come the flying beer cans again. Dad stopped his song and told the audience, "Look, I can't drink them that fast."

The fans laughed and, more important, stopped chunking beer at us.

"They weren't throwing them *at* you," Dad told me. "They were throwing them *to* you."

When Willie went on, the throwing commenced again.

One night in 1978, we were playing at Caesar's Palace in Vegas, without Willie. He and his wife, Connie, came to the show, and he walked up to me in the back and said, "Hey, boy, do you work for Waylon?" I didn't like him calling me "boy." He should have known my name, because we'd been doing shows together for at least a couple of years. Worse than feeling disrespected, I was on drugs and alcohol.

"Yes," I answered Willie.

"My car's in the fire lane back there," he told me. "Would you mind parking it for me?"

"No problem," I said.

Now, I have to admit that I've exaggerated this part of the story in the past by saying I drove Willie's Mercedes across town, parked it, and caught a cab back. Truthfully, I only took it to the most remote corner of the Caesar's parking lot that I could find. I'd say it was a least a quarter-mile walk back for me, but it was worth it. I found Willie, handed him his keys, and went back to work.

At about 3 A.M., I was in my hotel room, winding down from that night's work. The phone rang, and it was Dad. "Terry, Willie's up here in my room and says somebody that works for me parked his car. The way he's describing the person, it sounds like you. Did you park Willie's car?"

"Yeah, I parked it," I told my dad.

"Willie's looked everywhere for it and can't find it," he said. "Where is it?"

I told Dad where I'd parked the car.

"What the hell did you park it there for?"

"Tell him not to call me 'boy' again," I said.

Dad burst out laughing.

Willie found his car, and he never called me "boy" again. He's also never brought up the car with me. One of my sons once asked Willie about it, and Willie told him, "I don't remember a lot from those days. But if your dad said it happened, I'm sure it happened."

Willie's just lucky I didn't steal the joint in his ashtray. I eyed that joint a long time.

Those were good times touring with Willie's crew. However, we had to slow down our work because of Willie's crew. Our crew was incredible. We had to have been able to unload and load as fast as any crew in the music business. Unfortunately, Willie's crew wasn't one of the fastest around, and in order to keep from embarrassing them, Dad told us we had to slow down and finish loading closer to when the other crew was done. We hated that, because the rule for the crew was that until the truck was locked, we couldn't go out and play. In hanging out with Willie's crew, we were surprised to hear that they weren't playing to full houses. We were used to having sellouts when Dad was with Willie and when we were out on our own. But apparently that wasn't the case for Willie's crews, because they would talk about how much they liked being with Dad and playing to big crowds.

At times Willie's career would be appearing to drop a little, and he'd cut a duet with Dad that would provide him a boost. I know that Dad loved helping Willie out, because they were so close and he really liked Willie as a musician. Every musician's career goes through peaks and valleys, and Dad just so happened to be in places where he could offer his friend a boost. Dad and Willie once came up with the idea for an album called *Where There's a Willie, There's a Waylon*, but that one didn't get done.

There was no question that when Dad and Willie got together, great music would result. Good songs always, always, always, start with good writing. Beyond that, Dad and Willie sang together so much that they developed this chemistry that can't be manufactured. Their voices seemed to fit together naturally. To this day, it's just hard to beat a good song by Dad and Willie.

Willie wanted to make Austin, Texas, the new Nashville and move all the awards shows, recording studios, and artists there. Dad knew that wouldn't happen. Nashville was Nashville, the music capital of country music. Thanks to Willie, though, Austin did become the live music capital of the world.

14

BUSTED

Dad's drug use had worsened after Buddy Holly died. Following his move to Nashville, it peaked. It was nothing for Dad to stay awake three consecutive days, and the longest stretch I knew about was nine days. Pills were his drug of choice, but after Elvis Presley overdosed, the authorities cracked down on the doctors who had been supplying pills in Nashville.

Like many other artists in Music City, Dad got his pills from a Dr. Snapp who lived right off Music Row. Dr. Snapp had a chest of drawers in his house filled with Desoxyn pills. He'd scoop a bunch out of a drawer, sell them to you, and you were on your way. But after Elvis's death shut down the pill supply, along came cocaine.

Dad did $1,500 of coke per day. And it wasn't that way for a short period of time, either. From the time he started drugs until he quit, he was pedal to the metal. His supplier would fly out on a Learjet to where Dad was and drop him off a pound of the uncut stuff straight from Colombia for something like

$30,000. I'm pretty sure Dad was paying for the cost of using the jet, too. As far as I know, Dad was his supplier's only client.

Dad would take a quarter ounce of cocaine, a gram of speed or crank, and a Quaalude, and put everything in a grinder. You have to be pretty high to grind up a Quaalude, because those pills are hard as heck. Dad would sift his mix and then grind it again. Then he'd put his mix in an aspirin bottle that he stored inside a cigarette pack along with a short straw. Dad would carry the loaded cigarette pack on the inside of his vest, and he got to the point where he could take a bump without anyone seeing him do it. Actually, a bump is what the rest of us did. Dad would snort so much that we called it doing a *thump*.

He would take shortened McDonald's straws, which were wide, and pump them up with about an inch of coke inside. He'd put a straw in each nostril every fifteen minutes for about three days at a time. One year for Dad's birthday, CoCo and I stole a straw dispenser from Arby's and gave it to him.

When Dad would load up a straw for someone else, he'd keep the straw in the crook of his fingers, stick it down into the bottle, and wrap his little finger over it so nothing would fall out, and then hand it to you. I couldn't see how much was in there, but when I snorted it, I'd find out. We never knew what was going to come out of that straw when Dad handed it to you, but we took it anyway. Then he'd encourage us to do the other nostril so we wouldn't be "lopsided and walk around in circles." Once CoCo took a bump from Dad in his office, and when he snorted, his head slammed back against the door. CoCo slid down the door like he was in a cartoon and laid there on the floor, passed out. Dad just said, "He'll come to in a minute."

Like Dad told me, the first time you did cocaine was the best. The rest of the time, you were just chasing that first experience. His song "Lookin' for a Feeling," which opens with the line "I'm lookin' for a feeling that I once had with you," was about cocaine. Dad spent a lot of years looking for that feeling.

He seemed to have no fear of getting busted. He felt ten foot tall and bulletproof. Cocaine made me paranoid. The big joke was that when I did a bump, I'd be on the lookout through the peephole all night long, and they'd never take me alive.

"Why are you paranoid?" Dad would ask me. "They're going to catch you anyway."

The only "don't" Dad gave me concerning drugs was "Don't get the stuff off the street." After Dad quit drugs in 1984, his doctor told him that for someone who had snorted coke as long as him, his nostrils were in incredible shape. "That's because I had the good stuff," Dad said.

Dad bought the pure coke and told me he wanted me to get my drugs from him. I didn't always do that, though. It felt weird asking my dad for drugs all the time, so I tapped other sources. Plus, I liked pot, and Dad wouldn't keep that around.

For six years on the road I roomed with Baja Bob. Dad would sneak down the hall and tell us, "Your hall smells like pot. You need to cut it out." At one point, he split Fletcher and me up because there was too much crazy in our room. The party always seemed to gravitate to our room, where it was a free-for-all. But we weren't kept apart for long, because the crazy just spread into two rooms instead of being confined to one. To contain the crazy, Dad told us to go ahead and start rooming together again.

Fletcher had left ZZ Top to come work for Dad. About

three weeks after joining us, he told me, "I quit working for ZZ Top because it just got too crazy on the road with them. I thought working for a country act would be less crazy. I'll be damned if you guys aren't crazier than they are."

Don't Mess with Julie

One night during a break between road trips in the late '70s, my sister Julie was at the Gold Rush, one of the clubs on what was called the Rock Block in Nashville. A Hager twin from *Hee Haw* started hitting on Julie, who was twenty, and she made it clear she wanted nothing to do with him. He turned to walk away, and after taking a couple of steps turned back around and said that he didn't really want to go out with her anyway.

"The dog on *Hee Haw* makes more money than you," he told her.

That pissed Julie off.

"What does income have to do with anything?" she shot back at him.

Julie had a beer mug in her hand. From the result of her ensuing throw, I'd say Julie had the arm strength to be a major-league pitcher but lacked the necessary control. The mug sailed directly over the Hager twin's shoulder and struck the plate glass window at the front of the club. The mug didn't shatter the glass; it pierced the glass, leaving in its wake a hole like a bullet might. Good thing Julie missed, because she might have killed him if she had connected.

A security guard grabbed Julie, and the club owner rushed

over to whisper to the guard. He let go of Julie. The owner must have informed the guard that he was holding Waylon Jennings's daughter. Word got back to the twin, too, and he called Dad to apologize.

"You don't need to apologize to me," Dad told him. "You need to apologize to her. She'll whoop your ass."

Julie could have, and she would have.

On another break, Dad squeezed in a recording session between trips. I much preferred setting up equipment on the road to being in the studio. Dad tried to interest me in recording and mixing, but hearing the same people play the same notes over and over bored me to tears.

During a morning recording session, I was walking on Seventeenth Avenue between the studio and Dad's office. A yellow Cadillac pulled up alongside me, and inside was George Jones.

"What are you doing?" he asked me.

"Just getting some air," I said.

George got out of his Cadillac and opened the trunk. He had a bunch of two-gram vials of cocaine inside, and he handed me one. He also had a bottle of Jack Daniel's in the trunk, but George wasn't much into giving away his liquor.

I looked down and noticed that his license plate was a piece of cardboard with "GEORGE" handwritten on it. I asked about the plate.

"I had vanity plates with 'GEORGE' on them, but every time a tourist sees them, they steal them," he said. "So I put cardboard on there instead. The cops tell me to get real license plates, but I am getting tired of replacing them."

Flushing the Evidence

We were up north in August 1977—I want to say in Minnesota, but I'm not sure about that—and had two or three days off. Dad and Richie flew back to Nashville to go into the studio with Hank Williams Jr., who was cutting "Storms Never Last," which Jessi had written.

Around that time a guy who worked for Neil Reshen had made a huge mistake when setting up a trip to Jamaica for a young girl with brain cancer for whom Dad wanted to do a good deed. Dad let the guy have it over the phone. To make amends, the guy decided to send Dad about an ounce of cocaine through a private delivery service. For some reason, an employee with the delivery service became suspicious of the package and opened it. Sure enough, there was a second package inside with an ounce of coke, and the Drug Enforcement Agency was called in.

A DEA agent left two or three grams in the bag and confiscated the rest. The package was then shipped to Nashville. The guy who had sent the coke told Dad's secretary that an important package would be arriving at the Nashville airport. She picked up the package and took it back to the studios next to Dad's office. Dad took the package into the studio area, opened it, saw what was inside, and went back to work. Next thing you know, DEA agents were coming through the doors and into the control room where Richie was working. Richie had foresight enough to keep his hand on the call button, which allowed Dad in the recording area to hear everything that was going on. Dad grabbed the package and tossed it behind him.

Dad and Richie kept working, and Dad recorded harmony for the song while Richie tried to buy time in the control room. After Dad finished singing, he walked into the control room, and Richie played back the music for him like they were alone in the room. When the music stopped, one of the agents told my dad they had a warrant. Dad looked it over and noticed that the warrant listed him as the owner of the studio. Dad owned the office next door but was leasing the studio, and that made the warrant invalid.

The agents had to hang around while a proper warrant was secured. Meanwhile, Dad and Richie went back to work, in more ways than one. Dad had pills and a couple of vials in his pockets. He emptied his pockets on his way back to recording another track. Richie then came into the sound room to adjust Dad's microphone, and Dad told him where he'd tossed the package containing the drugs.

Richie went into the drum room to lay down a drum track. He dropped one bag of coke down through a crack in the wall in the drum room. Then with Dad creating a distraction, Richie was somehow able to sneak the second bag into the bathroom and flushed it down the commode. The agents heard the flush and later found the emptied bags. They had not found the two-gram vial that Dad had forgotten he had placed behind a lyrics sheet on a music stand. Dad and his secretary were arrested.

Meanwhile, back on the road, my sister Julie was traveling with us. We were in the hotel burning a few when I received a phone call from Tom Bourke, a crew member who doubled as my archnemesis. Tom and I bumped heads all the time.

"Have you heard?" he asked.

"Heard what?"

"Your dad just got busted back in Nashville," he informed me with a bit too much glee in his voice.

"What?" I asked.

Bourke repeated the news and laughed.

I hung up and told Julie, "Dad got busted in Nashville, and Bourke thinks it's funny. So we're fixing to go whip Bourke's ass."

We ran down to Bourke's room and started kicking at his door. Julie went down the hall and picked up a room-service tray that had been left outside a room and grabbed a butter knife. We tried to chisel our way into Bourke's room, screaming at him the whole time. Bourke called Dad, and Dad called Deacon, who came and dragged us down the hall, still kicking and screaming.

"This ain't no time for ruckus," Deacon told us. "That son of a bitch thinks it's funny. He's gonna get his ass whipped. We'll whip it later, not now."

The next morning, Dad and his secretary were arraigned on charges of conspiracy and possession of cocaine with intent to distribute. Of course, Dad's court appearance drew a big media crowd. Richie tried to shield Dad from a television camera and wound up hitting the cameraman with a soda can. That got Richie arrested for assault and battery.

Dad hired big-time lawyers Jay Goldberg and Elliott Sager from New York City. Charges against the secretary were dropped, and after a preliminary hearing, charges against

Dad were dropped without prejudice. Behind the scenes, the prosecutor told Dad that because of the bad warrant they had nothing on him, and that if he wouldn't say anything about what had happened, the charges would be dropped. Dad wrote a song called "Don't You Think This Outlaw Bit's Done Got Out of Hand" that included the line, "They came pounding through the back door in the middle of our song."

Despite that ordeal, Dad wasn't paranoid about another drug raid taking place. Some of us were, though, and we took steps to be ready. There was a window in the studio that faced out toward Dad's office and another at the right of the front door from which we could see across and down the street. The crew would make sure a person was stationed at each window every time we were recording in the studio.

Beak, Dad's co-road manager, was the most paranoid. When he'd been up for a few days, he would swear he could see people in the trees across the street who were trying to catch us with drugs. Once, he kept a pair of binoculars up to his eyes for so long and so tightly that when he lowered the binoculars, he had bruises around both eyes.

A portable office building was moved in across the street, and even though we tried to convince Beak that a publishing company was in that office, he swore to high heavens that the portable was set up by the FBI to watch us.

Even though we posted sentries at the windows, we didn't have an action plan in case of another raid. We all knew the bathroom's location, and that had worked the first time. If the studio was attacked, we would flush and figure out what to do from there.

15

A BUNCH OF ANGELS

Perhaps hiring bodyguards from the Hells Angels Motorcycle Club contributed to Dad's offstage Outlaw image. Based on the perception that came with traveling with members of Hells Angels, there is no telling how many stores we were alleged to have knocked over after we left a town.

Deacon Proudfoot and Ray Baker, whom we called "Boomer," traveled with us as bodyguards. In the flatlands of Texas where I grew up, Deacon—a big bear of a guy at about six foot three and three hundred pounds—would have qualified as a mountain. If you pissed Deacon off, he'd knock the crap out of you. But he'd first issue you a warning.

Boomer was smaller than Mount Deacon, skinny with scraggly hair. He wore false gold teeth. Boomer was different from Deacon in that he'd let someone go on for a while until he'd had enough. Boomer carried a cane he called Herbie. The handle had a big brass skull with a diamond for one eye. The other eye was missing, and he liked to say, "Herbie always has an eye out for you." Boomer would beat the crap out of people with Herbie. He also could whip out some karate if he chose to. The problem with Boomer, unlike Deacon, is that he didn't warn those who foolishly decided to mess with him when he'd had enough of them. He had a clear way of communicating that to them, but it was too late for that person to change his ways, if you know what I mean.

We played once a year, sometimes twice, in Jackson Hole, Wyoming, at the Million Dollar Cowboy Bar, one of my favorite places. I don't know whether it was always winter when we went there, but it sure seemed that way. One time I walked out of the restaurant next door and by the time I made it into the bar, my breath had caused icicles to hang from my beard.

On one trip to Jackson Hole, we went to the bar the night before the show, and one drunk cowboy started giving Boomer a hard time. The cowboy was unknowingly running out the meter on Boomer's patience when Deacon walked over and advised him to stop messing with Boomer. The guy opted not to follow Deacon's advice, and Deacon issued a rare second warning. "I'm telling you, you don't want to mess with this guy," he said. The cowboy continued on until Deacon grabbed the back of his shirt and belt, picked him up, and threw him out of the bar.

The bar had two plate-glass-window doors, and when the flying cowboy hit the door, he went through the window and landed on the broken glass. Needless to say, he got cut up pretty good.

C. A. Poindexter, the bar's owner, showed up and asked Deacon, "What'd you do that for?"

"It's your fault," Deacon said.

"How's that?" a befuddled C.A. asked.

"Nobody throws anyone *into* a bar, they throw them *out*," Deacon told him. "Your doors are swinging wrong."

When we returned the next year, C.A. had the doors swinging out instead of in.

As famous as Dad was, Deacon and Boomer had to deal with threats constantly. Most of them weren't serious, but, of course, they had to be treated that way. One that was serious came from the Outlaws Motorcycle Club, a rival of Hells Angels that wanted to become bigger than the Angels. That brought the Outlaws our way, because they thought they would earn more street cred if they could prove the Angels could not protect my dad and his family.

Unbeknownst to me, the Outlaws had put out a hit on a member of our family. The target had to be Dad, Jessi, or me, because we were the three on the road together at the time. We were in Florida, and some of us were partying in my room. Deacon always stayed on Dad's floor, and on this night, Boomer was outside my door wearing a long, leather slicker. It was summertime, and it was hot and humid—not exactly ideal slicker weather.

I asked Boomer four or five times if he wanted to come into the room and join us, and he said no each time.

After the party had wound down, around eight o'clock in the morning, only Baja Bob and I were in the room. I opened the door to see Boomer still standing there. I asked if he had been there all night, and he said yes. I asked why, and that was when he told me about the hit on us. Then he opened his slicker to show me that he was carrying guns and knives, and

I'm pretty sure I saw a grenade in there, too. Boomer had a complete arsenal inside that slicker.

I thanked him for the protection and told him I wished he had told me about the hit so I could have been more low-key.

Deacon and Boomer didn't mess around. I can't think of anything, or anyone, that they feared.

We were playing in Los Angeles in 1977, and Lynyrd Skynyrd was playing there at the same time in a different venue. From there, we were both going to Tulsa, Oklahoma, to play at Willie's picnic. The day after that, we were scheduled to play outside of San Francisco and they were playing in Oakland. Our groups decided to charter a commercial airline together and split the bill.

On the flight to Tulsa, it was announced over the intercom that there was a poker game going on at the front of the plane. My dad's road manager looked at Dad, and Dad looked at me.

"How much?" Dad asked me.

"Five hundred will start me," I told him, because I had $200 or $300 on me. "If I need more, I'll go to $1,000, and if I can't beat them with $1,000, then I don't need to be playing with them."

Dad's road manager gave me the money, and I walked to the front.

Lynyrd Skynyrd's guys looked at me and one of them said, "You can't afford to play poker with us."

I reached into my pocket and proved that I could afford the game.

"There's more where this came from," I informed them.

Then they laughed at me. I was nineteen or twenty at the time, and they said, "You're too young to play poker."

That set me off, and I started cussing them up a storm. Dad

sent Deacon to retrieve me, and Deacon started dragging me away from the game saying, "Don't start nothing on the way there. We'll take care of it on the way back."

We did our shows in Tulsa and boarded the plane for the flight to the Bay Area. Skynyrd's guys were wanting to be friends now, and one of them showed us a brand-new minitelevision.

"Look at our new toy," he proudly said.

"That's nice," Deacon told him, and then he picked up the TV and smashed it against the inside wall of the plane. Deacon and Boomer started giving them all kinds of trouble until Skynyrd's guys went up to the first-class section and closed the curtain to get away from Deacon and Boomer.

There is honor among road crews. We understand each other's jobs and we take care of each other. When our plane landed on the West Coast, we offloaded our gear together. When we came across something that belonged to the other band, we'd set it off to the side for them. We divided everything out and went on our separate ways.

As were setting up for our show, we noticed that our silver case of piano pickups was missing. One of us called Skynyrd's crew and asked if they had our missing pickups. We described the case, down to the number and stickers that were on it.

"No, we don't have anything like that," they told us.

"Are you sure?" we asked. "It was on the plane when we left Tulsa."

"No, we don't have it," they assured us.

"Look," we told them, "it's not that we don't trust you. But we have some friends in Oakland, and we're going to have a couple of them come over and look around, and maybe they can spot it where y'all can't. It'll be real easy to recognize them. They'll be on motorcycles, and it'll say 'Hells Angels' on their backs."

When the motorcycles pulled into the Coliseum entrance, our case of piano pickups was sitting in the middle of the parking lot, miraculously found, and ready for pickup.

Avoiding Arizona

Not even Hells Angels could help Dad in Arizona, though.

We used to have to circumvent the state during tours, because Dad refused to pay alimony to Lynne. I'm not exactly sure of the amounts, but I believe Dad was supposed to be paying about $1,000 a month for child support for Tomi Lynne and $500 per month in alimony. As Tomi Lynne's eighteenth birthday neared and the child support would stop, Lynne had those amounts flipped.

Dad had no problem paying for Tomi Lynne's child support. He loved Tomi Lynne and made sure she was provided for. But he had a major problem with Lynne's alimony. Lynne never remarried; she was content to live off Dad.

Arizona had agricultural inspection stations at its borders to prevent fruit from outside the state coming in and possibly bringing pests. (Although on one visit with our grandparents, we did smuggle in a yellow watermelon.) The inspectors had received BOLOs to be on the lookout for Dad because he wasn't paying alimony. He would have been arrested on the spot if he tried to go through an inspection station. Dad didn't play Arizona for a long time, because it would have cost him more than he wanted to pay to enter the state.

Before Arizona became a do-not-enter state, we played Mr. Lucky's in Phoenix in 1975. The production manager told me a woman and girl were at the door of the venue, and that the woman was claiming she was Dad's ex-wife and the girl was their daughter. I took a look and, sure enough, it was Lynne and Tomi Lynne.

I told the production manager that the woman had to leave but that the little girl could stay. The production manager said he'd take care of it for me. Lynne told him that if they both couldn't stay, they'd both leave. Her strategy failed, and they both left. They came back later that night, and Lynne told my dad, "I'd really like to see Terry and Buddy." Dad knew that we wouldn't be nice to her because of how she had treated us, so he told her, "You really wouldn't like to see them."

Tomi Lynne moved to Nashville near the end of 1989, after Lynne had passed away, and reunited with the family. Tomi Lynne was twenty-five, and at first Julie and Bud weren't happy to have her around. I was a little cold to her myself. With time, our relationships improved. But for a while, every time Tomi Lynne would bring up her mother, Julie would go off. I wouldn't, but I also wouldn't defend Lynne.

One night at a bar when we were out on the road, Tomi Lynne asked why Julie talked so badly about her mother.

"When we were kids, Lynne wasn't the best mom to us," I told her. "But I can guarantee you this: If you don't bring up your mother, no one will talk bad about her."

Tomi Lynne quit bringing Lynne up, and we all got along fine.

16

GOOD OL' BOYS

In 1978, Dad accepted an offer to become part of a television show titled *The Dukes of Hazzard*. The show, which was scheduled to debut the following January on CBS, would be about a down-home family in the fictitious Hazzard County, Georgia, and their run-ins with the conniving county commissioner and his equally inept law enforcement personnel.

Dukes of Hazzard was inspired by the movie *Moonrunners*, for which Dad had served as the narrator (officially, the "Balladeer") and wrote the soundtrack. During talks of turning the movie into a TV series, creator Gy Waldron—the screenwriter for the film, too—said it would be a deal breaker if my dad would not play the Balladeer. Dad also was asked to write and perform the show's theme song and the filler, or background, music.

Dad had a couple of concerns about doing *Dukes*. For one, he did not know how he would be able to fill the Balladeer role given how much he was touring. The show's executives told him that they would send him a script and he could find a local studio on the road and record himself reading the lines in different inflections. The producers would then edit in his parts. Second, he was a little apprehensive about doing television. He believed that if people could hear him for free on TV, they wouldn't buy tickets to his shows. He feared overexposure would cause fans to burn out on him.

In the end, Dad decided to take on the *Dukes of Hazzard* job, and that turned out to be a shrewd move, because he made $25,000 an episode and expanded his fan base. "Theme from *The Dukes of Hazzard* (Good Ol' Boys)" was his only single to go gold, by selling 500,000 copies.

In the first season, the show opened with two seconds of a tight shot of an anonymous man playing an acoustic guitar. Before the second season, Dad was offered more money to redo the shot with his own hands playing his guitar. After the first season, the show opened with a shoulders-down shot of Dad that faded into video of a General Lee jump and then Dad would begin singing the familiar, "Just'a good ol' boys / Never meaning no harm..." Dad stopped providing the filler music after the first season. The show's early popularity meant raises for the cast, and the money had to be spread around. Dad didn't mind, because making the filler music had turned out to be a pain in the butt.

To this day, I watch reruns of the show to hear Dad say lines like, "Now Uncle Jesse, he don't know who to chase, so he's just following the smoke." I can always tell how long Dad had been out on the road when he recorded his lines by how strong or how hoarse his voice was.

In the album version of "Good Ol' Boys," which he released in 1980, Dad changed the ending lyrics to "You know my momma loves me, but she don't understand they keep a showing my hands and not my face on TV."

Despite that last line, he didn't enjoy acting much. He made a few movies, and most of the time Willie or Cash had talked him into taking on those roles. Acting involved a whole lot of *hurry up and wait*, and Dad's approach to life was more of *Let's get this done and move on to the next item*. When Dad went to doctors, he had a five-minute rule: If he wasn't taken to the exam room within five minutes of his arrival—or, once he was in a room, if the doctor took more than five minutes to see him—he'd split.

Dad made only one on-camera appearance, in the final season of the *Dukes of Hazzard*, playing himself in the episode "Welcome, Waylon Jennings." Still, Dad stayed with the show all seven seasons, but at the end, I think it was beginning to run its course for him.

Although he recorded his lines away from where the show was filmed, he enjoyed the people associated with the show when he was able to spend time with them. Of the actors, we saw Tom Wopat, who played Luke Duke, the most. He started his own country music career and came to a lot of Dad's shows. I'd always call him Luke, and that bothered him. He'd tell me, "My name's Tom. Would you call me Tom?" I'd say, "Okay, Luke." If I could see him today, I'd have to ask his forgiveness. I was trying to be funny, but now I recognize I was being a prick.

John Schneider (Bo) showed up at a few shows, and we saw Catherine Bach (Daisy) a few times, too. I was a big fan of hers until I met some six-foot-tall guy who turned out to be her husband, dashing my hopes of ever being with Daisy Duke. Of the Duke family actors, Denver Pyle (Uncle Jesse) made it to the fewest of our shows, but he and Dad were good friends via telephone.

Dad had one of the numerous General Lee cars used on the show. He would let Shooter and my son, Josh, play in it as they grew up, and he'd take them for rides, too. That car was loud. I never drove the General Lee, although I did sit inside it. I didn't have to crawl through the window like the Duke boys, because the doors opened.

One effect of being on *Dukes of Hazzard* was that Dad's music was introduced to more kids than before, and that pleased him. We hadn't seen many kids at Dad's shows before, but when he did spot a kid, he liked to invite them backstage. Dad loved kids because they were honest. He said, "Kids don't care who you are. To a kid, you're either funny or you're not. Kids don't laugh at someone's jokes because they think they need to impress that person."

Being a star, Dad had too many people telling him what they thought he wanted to hear. That's why Dad appreciated a kid's honesty. But once the kids hit puberty, of course, then to him they became just like the rest of us.

"The Box"

Back when I was about ten or so, Julie, Buddy, and I came up with the term "the box." It was a figurative box, not a literal one, and was used to describe whomever Dad was upset or disappointed with. I recall many times when we weren't sure whether one of us was in the box or not. But Julie and I were in the box more than Buddy was. Once Jessi and Jennifer came along, Jennifer was rarely in the box.

There was one time, however, when she was big-time in the box.

It was 1979, and Jennifer was fifteen. Dad and Jessi called Julie, Buddy, and me over to their house. Julie and Buddy wanted to know what I had done wrong.

"I don't know," I told them.

So we're there with Dad, Jessi, Jennifer, and a heavyset guy named Pete. I was thinking, *What's going on here?*

Jessi began talking.

"We just want to tell you that Jennifer's pregnant," she said.

No way! She's fifteen!

"We took them out to Will Campbell's and they were married last night," Jessi continued.

We knew Will well. He was a preacher and close friend of Dad's who traveled with us frequently. Yeah, Dad was drugged out and taking a preacher on the road with him. Will liked to help out wherever he could. He especially liked to make us sandwiches, so we called him Hop Sing, after the cook in *Bonanza*.

Jessi apologized for not being able to tell us in time for us to attend the ceremony.

Dad and Jessi recorded the ceremony on a cassette tape and invited us to their house so we could listen together. So we sat there and listened to Jennifer and Pete exchange their vows on tape, relieved that it was Jennifer in the box instead of one of us for a change.

Babysitting Shooter

Shooter came along on May 19, 1979, the only child Dad and Jessi had together. Shooter's given name is Waylon Albright, making him a W.A. Dad was close to forty-two and Jessi was a week shy of her thirty-sixth birthday when Shooter was born, and he wanted to have Shooter around all the time. Jessi and Shooter traveled with Dad, and they brought Maureen Rafferty along to help take care of Shooter. Maureen was the governess. She was Shooter's nanny on the road and chief of staff at home. As Dad and Jessi's bodyguard, Boomer also was bodyguard by proxy to Maureen and Shooter. I'll never forget looking out my hotel window—when Shooter was three or four—to see little Shooter running the sidewalks with a three-hundred-pound nanny and a Hells Angel bodyguard carrying a cane in full pursuit.

Dad was so proud of Shooter and would introduce him at shows. He'd done the same with me when I was younger, but I hated it. Dad knew that, and sometimes I think he introduced me to an audience just to get under my skin.

When Shooter was less than a year old, I was doing my drum tech job on a trip that Maureen didn't make. I was onstage when Boomer ran up to me. Boomer normally brought Jessi onstage for her duet with Dad, but that night he came alone and said I was needed immediately on the bus. I told Richie I had to leave and asked Baja Bob to take care of the drums.

When I got to the bus, Jessi told me she needed me to watch Shooter while she joined Dad onstage. I didn't know anything about babysitting. Jessi hurriedly told me, "Here's a diaper and here's a bottle. If he cries, one of these will fix it."

The very minute I was left alone with Shooter, he started crying. I tried the bottle, and that didn't work. I felt his diaper and, yep, he was wet. I had never changed a diaper. I managed to get the new one on, but it was too loose. I pulled the sticky tabs off and tried to put them back on tighter, only to learn that you get only one shot with those darned tabs.

I looked around for another diaper or a diaper bag, but couldn't find either. Then my luck turned. On the table where Dad played cards sat a beautiful roll of duct tape—a roadie's best friend. I put the diaper back on Shooter tighter and placed a strip of duct tape around his waist, making sure not to touch his skin. The diaper still was baggy. So I ran another strip of tape around the crotch. The diaper was secure, and Shooter wasn't crying. We were good!

When Jessi came back to the bus, she got such a laugh out of my duct tape artistry that she left Shooter taped up until Dad came to the bus after his show. Dad laughed, too, and I never had to babysit again.

Dad and Jessi asked Julie, Buddy, and me to avoid trying to be an influence on Shooter. I told them I was fine with that and that I wasn't going to tell him anything. "But if he asks me questions," I said, "I'm not going to lie."

Dad and Jessi could live with that.

Though I am twenty-two years older than Shooter, he has always been drawn to me for some reason. I'm surprised he didn't hate my guts as a kid, or fear me.

I am a humongous Dallas Cowboys fan, and one of our family rules was that if we were all in town and the Cowboys were playing, we gathered at Dad and Jessi's to watch together.

One game, Shooter was still young enough that he was in a walker. He'd roll up to me and I'd fiddle with him a little bit in a way that would entertain him without distracting me from the game. Then when the ref would miss a call or something bad would happen to my Cowboys, I'd stand up and cuss at the TV. That scared Shooter, and he'd let out a loud scream. I'd apologize, and Jessi would come running into the room to see what was wrong. Dad would assure her everything was okay with Shooter, that it was just me yelling at the game.

Looking back, I'm surprised I didn't scar him for life over Cowboys games.

Shooter's godfathers are Johnny Cash and Muhammad Ali. I guess with godfathers from Christianity and the Nation of Islam, Dad and Jessi figured they had Shooter covered spiritually.

Ali attended Shooter's christening. Dad's favorite sport was boxing, and Ali was his favorite boxer. I met Ali at our house. Buddy, Baja Bob, and I were headed to the kitchen and there taking up our hallway were Ali and a big man I assumed was his bodyguard.

"I want you to meet Muhammad Ali," Dad said.

"Nice to meet you, champ," I said as we shook hands. "You're the greatest."

Ali had the softest hands I'd felt in my life. He had a gentle soul and talked softly, too.

Hillbillies in the White House

In the summer of 1980, Dad took Jessi, Shooter, and me to the White House to meet President Jimmy Carter. The election was coming up, and President Carter was up for reelection against California governor Ronald Reagan. He also was trying to get the hostages out of Iran.

Jessi looked pretty, as usual, in a nice blouse and jeans. Dad wore a nice shirt and his best blue jeans. I was twenty-three and chose to wear my best T-shirt and blue jeans. Jessi was a big John F. Kennedy fan, and she had one-year-old Shooter dressed in a Kennedy outfit.

We had to have looked like the Beverly Hillbillies walking into the White House. But we didn't mind; we had embraced being hillbillies. David St. John, a road crew member, had written a take-off of the theme song from *The Beverly Hillbillies* we all sang that included the lyrics,

Well, the first thing you know Waylon's a millionaire.
Kinfolks said, "Waylon move away from there."

Said "Nashville is the place you ought to be,"
So he loaded up his Caddy and moved to Tennessee.
Telecasters, singing stars....

A member of the president's staff gave us a special tour that regular White House visitors did not receive. He told us, "Now you've seen everything that the general public can't see. If you decide to return and take that tour, you can say you've seen the entire White House."

One of the places we visited was the president's bedroom. I looked under the bed, and they had clothes crammed underneath just like the rest of us do. I wanted a souvenir and saw a couple of brass dice that would have made for a good conversation starter. I picked them up and was about to slip them into my pocket when I felt like I had eyes all over me. I probably did, so I put them back.

We met the president and had lunch with the First Lady. We all liked our meat well done, and they brought out the rawest piece of meat I'd seen since that rack of lamb from Jessi's catered meal. I ate the whole thing. Dad couldn't believe it and asked why I ate the meat red.

"We're in the White House," I told him. "You don't send it back."

Buddy told me they had been served the same type of raw meat on a previous trip to the White House.

"I sent mine back," Bud said.

17

OUT OF CONTROL

I quit working for Dad in 1980 when I was twenty-three. I got mad at Richie over an incident in the studio, went home, and decided I'd had enough. My way of giving my notice was to not show up that evening to board the crew bus for the next trip. When someone from the office called, I told them I had quit.

I went to Dad's house early the next morning with my first wife, Kathy, to detail the circumstances. This was Dad and Jessi's "Southern Comfort" home in the Brentwood suburb south of Nashville. That house was large, and there was a good deal of distance from Dad's bedroom to the room we called the cave, where we were waiting on him.

Dad started cussing and screaming from his bedroom, stormed into the cave, and told me to get out of his house without allowing me a chance to explain why I had quit. We quickly left, and Kathy took me home and then promptly returned to try to talk to Dad.

Dad called me and told me, "You need to talk to Kathy and tell her to come home."

"That's your problem," I told him.

About an hour later, Kathy walked in the door. Dad and I didn't talk to each other for four or five months, until I called to tell him that he had a grandson.

With me out of a job, Kathy and I decided to move back to Texas, where we lived in a mobile home on a rented lot in Grand Prairie. During that time when Dad and I weren't talking, things went south with Dad's band. During my final six months on the crew, the drug problem had been spiraling out of control.

Dad didn't like crew or band members selling drugs on the road, not even to each other. Nor did he want his people buying drugs on the road, whether from strangers or from the network of suppliers they'd built up through the years. Yet at the same time, Dad couldn't supply everyone with drugs.

My dad would have a kilo of coke with him. The crew members could take care of themselves. We'd had our ways of staying supplied that the others didn't know about because what happened on the crew stayed within the crew. However, the band members began to feel like Dad was holding out on them, or suspected that he would give one person more than he would give another. That created jealousy among the band members.

He'd given me drugs when I'd asked, though. Baja and I would go to him and say, "It's been a rough one." Dad would dump some coke in a bag and say, "Y'all can split it up." We'd do the coke and then get some pot through the crew network.

It wasn't Dad's obligation to make sure everyone had drugs. But he also had those restrictive rules in place, and the band had to get drugs from somewhere while they were on the road.

The tension among the band and crew heightened. On stage, the shows were still good, but not as great as they'd been. The Waylors would kick off a show, and they'd be really into their set. Then Jessi would join the Waylors, and they'd be into their part with her, although not to the same level as with their set. Then after Jessi would leave, we would have a quick set change and Dad would come onto the stage, and it was like the Waylors were going through the motions for him. Don't get me wrong: Even on their worst night, they were still good. But I could see how the performances suffered. I don't know if what was taking place behind the scenes affected the crowds or not, because there didn't seem to be much attention paid to the audiences.

The boiling point came after I'd left and Dad decided, *Screw it, it's time to regroup.* Dad called the band members together and told them, "Individually, I love every one of you to death, but as a group, you piss me off. Everybody's fired."

Everybody except Moon and Jigger, that is.

Jigger—I'm sorry to say this, but he was a yes-man. Dad trusted Jigger and kept him through thick and thin. Jigger was a good guy, but I never trusted him as much as Dad did.

As far as Moon, you just don't fire Moon. (Although Dad later did, and I'll explain that.) Moon was Dad's hero. Dad had met him at the Golden Nugget in Vegas back in the '60s. He played steel for Buck Owens, Merle Haggard, Wynn Stewart, and Wanda Jackson before Dad hired him as part of the Waylors.

Mr. Moon, as we called him, could get away with things that other members of Dad's band couldn't. Dad had this evil eye he'd give someone if they did something wrong. When Dad gave you the evil eye, you'd feel like he was staring right through you and burning a hole in the back of your head. We all took that look seriously. Except Moon. He would just laugh at my dad, and there was nothing Dad could do about it.

Dad had one rule for the rest of us concerning Moon: Never give him the bus keys. Before Moon came to work with Dad, when he got good and drunk, he was known to steal cars, and even a bus or two, because he started missing his wife and wanted to get back home to her. So Dad told us that if Moon was drunk and asked for the bus keys, we were to walk him to the bus. Dad warned us that if he ever saw Moon with the keys, he'd fire the disobedient soul who'd given him the keys.

One time, Moon tricked his way into getting the keys. Moon was drunk and wanted to get home to Mrs. Moon. He got as far as a set of railroad tracks on which he happened to high-center the bus. The drivers had to go get the bus off the tracks. Dad never found out who had given Moon the keys.

Moon gave us a rule, too: If he passed out drunk, we were to carry him to the bus, put him in his bunk, and make sure to lay him on his stomach. He'd had a friend who got drunk, fell asleep on his back, threw up in his mouth, and drowned in his own puke. Moon had a fear the same would happen to him, so we always did as he wished when he passed out. The bunks were three high, and his was a middle bunk. He was a short guy, but he was surprisingly heavy when we lifted him up to his bunk.

Moon didn't look like the rest of us young, hippie-looking guys. He was always dressed to a T. But he got a kick from hanging out with us.

Once, we had a day off before a gig in New York, and some of us decided to go watch a Yankees game, because most of the guys loved baseball. I'm a huge football fan—the Dallas Cowboys are still America's Team!—but I had never been to a professional baseball game.

We sat up high in right field of Yankee Stadium, smack-dab in the middle of a bunch of diehard Yankee fans. Most of our guys were on LSD and drunk. I wasn't on LSD, because I never liked it. I was drunk with the others, though. When Yankees fans started getting on us about our long hair, we felt enough false bravery to give them a hard time back.

Moon was sitting right in front of us quietly watching the game. He turned around and said he wanted a beer, so we handed him one. When those fans saw that we were there with Moon, they were shocked. I remember one of them saying something along the lines of *The old guy is with the crazy ones*. After that, we all became friends. That was Mr. Moon for you—a man who was very easy to like, even for strangers and rowdy Yankees fans.

Mr. Moon was just a little sweetheart. He called people "sugar tit" all the time, as in "Hey, sugar tit." He could get a little ornery when drunk—just ornery enough to entertain us.

On another trip into New York City, I was getting back to the hotel after a show and I could hear Moon's distinctive, high-pitched voice coming from the bar. I went in and asked him what the problem was.

"It ain't my problem," he said. "It's that damn bartender."

The bartender was young and wore a befuddled look on his face.

"What seems to be the problem here?" I asked him.

"He's wanting beer and mater juice," the bartender said. "If he would tell me what mater juice is, I'd give it to him."

"He means *tuh-mey-toh* juice," I said.

The bartender got right to work getting beer and tomato juice for Moon.

I shot Moon a that's-all-you-had-to-do look.

Moon didn't give in, saying to me, "He's still a son of a bitch."

Moon could be that way. He was not going to say *tuh-mey-toh*; that Yankee bartender was going to have to learn to speak his way.

My favorite story about Dad and Moon took place, best I can remember, in Lubbock. Moon and my dad's brother Bo were really drunk and making tons of noise in the hotel parking lot. The cops showed up and handcuffed them.

Dad stepped out onto his balcony and called out, "What's going on down there?" The cops yelled back up to Dad that they were arresting Moon and Bo for public drunkenness. Dad shouted down to the cops, "The old man, let him go. But the other guy, you can take him on to jail." Moon looked up to Dad and said, "Screw you, Waylon! If he's going to jail, I'm going too." Dad said, "Okay, let them both go." The cops did, and Moon and Bo continued to raise havoc.

Back to Work with Dad

The first time I talked to Dad after he had kicked me out of Southern Comfort was in March 1981 when my first son, Whey, was born.

I called Dad. "You have a grandson," I told him.

Dad and Jessi came down to Grand Prairie to see Whey. They stayed in our home, and we had a good visit. It was as if nothing had happened between Dad and me.

I pointed out to Dad that I had kept my promise to Grandpa by making my first son a *W.A.* I was not going to give him the first name of Waylon or Willie. As I thought about other names that started with *W* none appealed to me. I would eat cereal out of a big bowl like Jethro Bodine, and I'd read the cereal boxes as I ate. I was reading the ingredients one day and came across "Whey."

That would make a cool name, I thought. *It's sort of like Waylon, but it's not Waylon. It's original. We'll name him Whey.*

Kathy was an Elvis Presley fan and chose Elvis's middle name for the *A*, with two *R*s in Arron.

A few months after Whey was born, Kathy became ill and had to go into the hospital. While I was there, the doctors noticed a cyst under my jaw and admitted me into the hospital to have it surgically removed.

On the day of the surgery, Dad called me and asked me to work for him again. I had a job with a mobile home company in Texas and had worked my way up to a foreman position.

I called my dad back the next day and told him that I was really doped up from my surgery and didn't want to go back to work with him.

When I went back to my job, still bandaged from the surgery, my boss raised a fuss about me not letting him know I would be missing work and fired me. I explained that because the doctors had performed surgery on me right away, the best I could do was to ask a neighbor and coworker to let him know what was going on. The boss backed down a little—he said he wouldn't fire me, but that I could no longer be a foreman and would lose the raises I had received as I'd worked my way up in the company.

That did it. I got Dad on the phone and told him I wanted to work with him after all. He told me that he had fired everyone except Moon, Jigger, and the crew, and that things were different from when I had left. He had a drum tech, but he said I could come back and "find things to do."

In my new role, I was sort of a road manager for a while and then a production manager for a period, but for the most part I filled in the gaps.

Hometown Crowd

Grandma Jennings had an idea for Dad to put on a show in Littlefield as a way to help out his hometown. In 1985, Dad scheduled the first one around his trip to Texas for Willie's picnic.

I never saw Dad more nervous than he was that day. He was

sweating bullets, afraid no one would show up. When I asked why, he said, "You have to realize, these people changed my diapers. They didn't like me as a kid." He never forgot how many people in Littlefield had said he was making a mistake in those early years trying to make a career in music and, in their opinion, forsaking his family.

As it turned out, a big crowd did show. A large area was sectioned off for family—the ones who had changed his diapers. The first show went off well enough that it became an annual event. He brought Cash with him—I believe it was the second or third year.

Dad grew frustrated with Littlefield, though. After the first year, police officers from surrounding areas were brought in to provide security for the large crowds. But businesses were shutting their doors the day of the event because the owners and employees wanted to go to the show. The purpose was to help the town make money, and the businesses weren't staying open with all the visitors rolling into town. My great-aunt Freda was an exception. She kept her restaurant open and made good money.

Littlefield put up a sign declaring it my dad's hometown. The first sign bore perhaps the worst picture of Dad available. He said the school teachers who hadn't liked him must have been in charge of selecting it. That sign was replaced by one with a better picture.

Dad was superproud of being from West Texas, but I don't think he had similar feelings for his hometown, even though he continued doing the Littlefield shows for free into the '90s. That criticism he had endured from people in the town when he was trying to make a go of it in music turned to jealousy after he became a star. He was very protective of his mother, and he didn't like anything that affected Grandma adversely. He started doing the Littlefield shows to put a little spotlight on her and to bring her some respect, which did happen. But when he felt like members of the Littlefield Arts and Heritage Committee began using her more than respecting her, Dad shut the shows down.

Good to the Last Show

Touring back in the '70s and '80s wasn't like it is today in the music industry. Nowadays, acts will do a tour of twenty-five to thirty days. Back then, it was constant touring, because that was what the record labels expected.

We'd be out on the road, and dates would get added as we went along. We would think we knew when we would be going home, and then we'd find out that we'd be staying out on the road longer than planned.

When we returned home from a trip, the first thing we did was unload the band gear into the studio. Dad would be waiting in the control booth for us, and he'd start right away on a recording session. Three of us on the crew would take shifts during the recording sessions, working a couple of days at a time so we could each get done what we needed to at home before hitting the road again.

The arenas and coliseums were great. But every once in a while there would be someone out in the middle of nowhere who wanted to put on a concert in a field. The setting would be cool, but the stage would be made up of fifty-gallon drums with plywood on them. The weight of the sound, lighting, and band equipment made those stages feel unsafe. We never had one of those makeshift stages fall in on us, but I was a nervous wreck when we were on them.

Dad once did a free show at a high school football field in Athens, Texas, and he brought a stage in so he could do the show right. When we disassembled the stage, the weight of the stage had created deep holes in the football field. Apologies to the Athens football team.

Dad was the first Nashville artist to land a corporate sponsor with the "Maxwell House Give 'Em a Hand" concert series in 1983 that benefitted children's charities. Dad, Jessi, and Jerry Reed were the headliners.

Funny thing was that it came down to either Maxwell House or Seagram's as the sponsor. We put on a show for each company. The Maxwell House people were drunk as all get out, and the Seagram's people were all drinking coffee.

Our biggest mistake was allowing Maxwell House to oversee the production. They took some guy who deserved a raise and made him the production manager. He didn't know what he was doing, and it took us a good couple of weeks to wrestle control away from him. We assured him that he'd get paid the same and receive the credit, but we told him to stay out of the way so we could get the shows done right.

Originally, the deal called for Dad and Jerry to swap out as closing act. About a week in, we noticed that when Dad closed, the house was full all night and when Jerry closed, people left after Dad had finished. A meeting was called, and it fell to me to say that the best thing for the tour would be for Dad to close every night.

Jerry had a habit of saying, "I've been in the business for twenty years and..." He started with that, and Dad interrupted, "I've only been in the business eighteen years, but I stayed up twice as long as you. So I'm closing."

Everyone left the room but me and Baja Bob. When we walked out, Jerry was waiting for us. He pointed to his face and told me, "Hit me right here. When you talk about me like you did in that meeting, you might as well hit me in the face."

"I won't hit you," I told him. "I didn't mean anything bad about it. Those are just the facts."

We finished the Maxwell House tour at Opryland. Hank Williams Jr. showed up with his girlfriend and asked about the tour and how the corporate sponsorship had worked.

"It's great because you get paid up front, before the tour," I told him. "But the one thing we learned is to make sure you keep control of your own production. Don't let them handle it—that's a pain in the butt."

I bumped into Hank's girlfriend four months later while listening to a band at Nashville's Bluebird Café, and she invited me over to her apartment. She had a brand-new Camaro, and the next morning we were driving it back to pick up Bud's car, which I had borrowed from him. I took a wrong turn leaving the apartment complex, and while backing up to correct my mistake, I jumped the curb and hit a water plug, leaving a hole in the back right quarter panel.

A few days later, Hank called and asked if I had wrecked his girlfriend's car.

"Yes, I did," I said.

"Are you going to pay for it?" he asked.

"No," I said. "You bought her insurance, didn't you?"

"What are you doing running around with my girlfriend?" he asked. "You're married."

"You're married, too," I reminded him.

That was followed by some cussing and a couple of phones being slammed. Hank and I didn't talk to each other for the next three years, until one night at Billy Bob's in Fort Worth, Texas. I saw Hank walk in, with his back to me. When he turned and saw me, he shot me a dirty look.

"Hank," I asked him, "how long are you going to stay mad over that girl? She's not even your girlfriend anymore. When are you gonna get over it?"

"You're right," Hank said. "Let's go get a drink."

We did, and we became buddies again.

18

A SOBER DAD

Dad quit drugs on March 31, 1984. I cite Jessi and Shooter as his main motivation.

He had just about run Jessi through the wringer. Shooter was four at the time, and he already knew he wanted to be like his dad when he grew up. That frightened Dad.

Jessi had been telling Dad that he couldn't quit drugs. I don't know if she was employing reverse psychology, but one of the best ways to get Dad to do something was to tell him that he couldn't do it.

He said nothing to me, the crew, or the band about his plans. Dad cut back his dates for a while to playing only on the weekend, to being what was called a weekend warrior. At that time, it wasn't uncommon to take a month off. All we knew was that we were taking April off and he would spend the month in Arizona. My thought was, *Good for him. He needs it.*

In fact, I thought everybody could use a break. The weekend

warrior schedule was tougher than all-out touring. We would go home and leave, go home and leave, and then we would have studio sessions mixed in. The pace didn't slow at all from before; it was just a different schedule that didn't have a rhythm. Plus, we were making the same money, even though the weekend warrior schedule strained us more.

Out in Arizona, Dad snorted cocaine one more time and that was it. He spent April sobering up, and near the end of the month, he took from the bus a briefcase with about a pound of coke inside and burned it in a bonfire. When Dad determined to do something, he did it, and that was how he kicked cocaine.

"Betty Ford didn't get me on this shit," he would say, "and she couldn't get me off it."

I learned about it along with the rest of the band and crew. When we got back together, Dad matter-of-factly told us, "I have quit drugs. I don't expect you all to quit drugs, but I would appreciate if you didn't do them around me." That was Dad's way of saying he wasn't going to dictate our lives, but it would be a respectful gesture on our part not to tempt him.

Dad told me that at the end of those thirty days, he could see more clearly. He looked at Jessi and noticed she was worn out, that she wasn't the energetic person he had married. No longer blinded by the drugs, Dad could see the hell he had put Jessi through.

I was pleasantly surprised by Dad's brief announcement. I knew the drugs had caused friction between him and Jessi. Plus, this was my dad, and I wanted him to live forever.

I'd also noticed over the years how they had struggled to

write off the drug habit. The drugs were a big expense, and writing them off proved difficult. I knew that his accountant had once had a Corvette built they named Shooter. The accountant was a wannabe NASCAR driver, and they took the Corvette to a track and slammed it into a wall. The parts in the car had been overvalued, and that was one way that drugs had been written off.

Drugs do funny things to you. I was the stereotypical user in that I thought the other person couldn't handle drugs as well as I could. When you're in that culture and you're feeling that those around you aren't bulletproof like you, you still don't try to get them to stop. You're just too high to know any better. We all were enablers, and the subject of quitting never came up. Even though I'd never told Dad he should quit drugs, I was very excited for him when he said he was through with them.

Dad avoided the band and crew more after that conversation. We would do stupid things on the crew, especially regarding our network for acquiring drugs on the road. We trusted people we shouldn't have, that was for sure. But somehow, we never got busted.

Dad stopping drugs didn't change anything within the crew. We tried our best to do fewer drugs, but we were arriving to work at 8 A.M. and not leaving until 2 A.M. the next morning. Then a few hours later, the cycle would start over. That was a pretty rough schedule without some "help," and it wasn't until later that some of us discovered the therapeutic benefits of a nap.

The band chemistry did change, however. J. I. Allison, the

drummer, left soon after, but that wasn't related to drugs. Jerry Gropp, an original Waylor that Dad had brought back after firing his old band, quit for what I thought were drug reasons. I don't think he could afford drugs, and Dad was out as a supplier.

The band was in constant change from that point.

Dad immediately began gaining weight after he stopped drugs, and that frustrated him to no end. He became swollen, not necessarily fat. When we Jenningses gain weight, we tend to have skinny legs, small butts, and big guts, and that was just what happened with Dad. He began following a healthier diet, becoming a fan of taco salads. When Maureen made tuna fish for him, she replaced the mayonnaise with picante sauce.

The new diet necessitated changes to the riders on top of our contracts for shows, and healthier recipes were sent ahead to the catering departments of venues. Although the dining options changed drastically, the liquor requests didn't. We still asked for three cases of Miller Lite, one case of Budweiser, two bottles of Jack Daniel's, one bottle of gin, a bottle of vodka, one bottle of red wine, and one bottle of white wine.

Dad, of course, didn't drink, so that all was for the band and the crew. Except for the wine, which was for Jessi, even though she didn't drink wine often.

Around the one-year anniversary of Dad quitting drugs, Johnny and June Cash threw Dad a sobriety party at their house in Hermitage, Tennessee. Willie Nelson couldn't make it, so he cut off two braids of his red hair and sent them to Dad as a gift. Dad kept those braids, and in 2014, they sold at an auction for $37,000.

Everyone at the party was supposed to do something comical. The best I could come up with was to introduce myself as though Dad and I had never met because he had been on drugs. That didn't go over well.

Robert Duvall, a pretty good singer himself, was there and reenacted a true, hilarious story from one of Dad's tours.

One night, Dad had come back to his and Jessi's room all showered up. Um-huh. He was getting undressed when Jessi asked, "Waylon, don't you think that poor girl would like her shirt back?"

Waylon looked down at the shirt he was removing and remarked, "I'll be damned. You don't know how much red looks like black in the dark."

Marylou Hyatt, Dad's office manager, reenacted a story from another tour.

We had decided to step up Jessi's part of the show and brought out plants and flowers to make her set look more feminine. One night during the set change from Jessi's to Dad's, a small tree was mistakenly left onstage. Dad walked out and a female voice from the front of the crowd shouted something. Then another and another repeated it. Dad couldn't make out what they were saying, so he stopped singing, the band stopped playing, and Dad asked, "What are you all trying to tell me?"

Almost in unison, the entire front of the crowd shouted, "Your fly's open!"

Dad turned around and tried to close his zipper, but couldn't. I was back at the sound board at the time and had the same view as the audience: It looked like Dad was peeing directly on that tree.

Dad didn't get his broken zipper up, and Jessi came out and placed a piece of duct tape over his crotch.

At the sobriety party, Marylou walked out wearing a Waylon vest and a fake beard. She stood there with a pair of pliers and tried repeatedly to pull her zipper up.

Gary Scruggs, a member of Dad's band, gave him an extendable mirror he could place on his guitar and make sure his fly was closed.

The Highwaymen

By 1985, Dad's sales with RCA had dropped. He was still selling albums, but the numbers weren't off the charts as they had once been. After twenty years with RCA, he decided that summer not to re-sign with them and wound up joining MCA Records.

At that time, a brainchild of Dad's was beginning to appear truly genius. Dad had brought Willie and Cash together and, seeking a fourth member to create a supergroup, they decided to bring aboard Kris Kristofferson. The four brought pieces of their own bands together, with Dad choosing Jigger on bass and Robby Turner on steel from his band.

The group's single "Highwayman" shot to number one on the charts, and their album by the same name went platinum. From that single, they became known as the Highwaymen.

At first Dad thought the Highwaymen would be a one-tour-and-done idea. As it turned out, the four of them toured the world and, over the next decade, produced three major albums and three singles that made the charts. The Highwaymen revitalized all their careers, and from my standpoint, I thought Dad being a part of that group really showed off his vocal abilities, especially his harmonizing.

I remember Kristofferson having a bit of a "Who, me?" reaction to being included in that group. I think he believed that Dad, Willie, and Cash were all bigger than him, but he was right up there with them.

Dad respected Kristofferson as a songwriter. In the early days, he was protective of Kris. I have memories of Kristofferson coming to our house quite a bit in the early '70s. He was a cool guy. When I was in the eighth grade and we were living in Donelson, he stopped by to see us with his girlfriend, who was tall and good-looking. I can't remember why, but Kris's girlfriend stayed with us for a week, and I hung to her like glue. Like I was going to steal away Kris Kristofferson's girl! I was thirteen then and full of hope.

I was a big Crosby, Stills, Nash, and Young fan, and before Kris's girlfriend left, she slipped into my black bedroom and left one of their records with a nice note she had written for me. Kristofferson wasn't around as much after he decided to get into the movie business, but it was good to see him again when the Highwaymen came together. He had cut back on his drinking by then, perhaps even completely.

There was a ton of mutual respect between Dad and

Kristofferson. They seemed to put each other on a pedestal that neither believed he belonged on.

My Turnaround

I didn't consider stopping drugs like Dad, and he didn't try to convince me to. Actually, my drug usage increased after Dad sobered up, to the point that in 1985 I was given the option of resigning my job with him or getting fired.

Baja Bob called me one day and asked my permission to order new equipment cases because the wheels on our cases were wearing out. Cases were expensive, and I told Baja that we could take the wheels off cases in our warehouse and place them on the ones we were using. The crew didn't like my idea and called Dad.

I'd been causing trouble with the crew, and Marylou Hyatt called me in and told me that my dad said I should quit or be fired. Because I was an asshole back then, I told Marylou I'd rather be fired than quit. To me, what difference would it make whether I quit or got fired? Would I be embarrassed that my dad fired me? Or would I be proud that I had quit? It made no difference to me.

At that point, my second son, Johnny, had been born, and I moved with Kathy and our two sons back to Texas and took a job with the same mobile home company I'd worked for previously. I got laid off from that job three months later. My wife hadn't worked since we'd married, and I told her that it was her turn to get a job. We both found work, but our marriage had pretty much been over for some time, even before we had moved back to Texas. She left me for another man and took our sons with her.

That was my rock-bottom.

My path back to respectability began with my current wife, Debra, who found me in the gutter and helped me get back up.

I met Debra, a very pretty blonde, on July 3, 1984, while we were in Austin for one of Willie's picnics. She had friends in Willie's circle, and Willie's sister—whom we called Aunt Bobbie—is the reason we are together.

I was pretty bad then, and my marriage to Kathy was basically over. Following Willie's pre-picnic banquet, I was drunk in the Wyndham Hotel bar. I didn't make a good first impression on Debra. The next night, after the picnic, we were in the same hotel lobby and bar area, and it was packed with everyone who had played the picnic and friends. A friend of mine, Kal Roberts, told me to take his seat at the horseshoe bar in the lobby. Immediately when I sat down, Debra turned sideways with her back to me. I leaned in front of her to apologize to the lady sitting next to her for my behavior the night before. I asked Debra if I had done something to offend her.

"I can't believe you can even talk," Debra told me. "I'm surprised you're not like that all the time."

"I hope not," I said to her.

Aunt Bobbie walked up and told Debra that their group was going back to a private area the hotel had set up for them in the restaurant and would be reopening the bar for them. As they walked away, Aunt Bobbie turned and said, "Terry, why don't you come with us?" I didn't hesitate to follow them.

That invitation was not what Debra wanted to hear.

Aunt Bobbie told Debra that I worked for Waylon Jennings, but Debra didn't know he was my dad. On the way from the bar to the restaurant, Debra asked Poodie from Willie's crew, "Who is this guy?"

"Groaner," Poodie answered, using the nickname Willie's crew had given me when we toured together. "You know Groaner?"

"No, I don't," Debra told him.

From Aunt Bobbie, Debra learned that my first name was Terry. She thought my name was Terry Groaner.

Fortunately, Aunt Bobbie told Debra that I was a good guy, and she agreed to go out on a date with me. I didn't tell Debra that I was technically married until our third date. She told me she wouldn't be seeing me again until I was no longer married. I told Debra—quoting from a Bob Seger song—"Someday, lady, you'll accompany me."

A year and a half later, I tracked Debra down through her parents. Her mother, Tony, was kind enough to give me Debra's work number, and I was able to convince Debra to go out with me again. Her father, Kermit, was a school superintendent. Considering all the trouble I had encountered during school, it was funny to me that I dated the daughter of a superintendent.

"I never saw that coming," my dad told me.

Debra convinced me over time that my friends weren't really my friends. When I quit hanging around them, my drug use began to decline. About a year and a half after Dad had quit drugs, I was off all the hard stuff and using pot only occasionally.

After being turned down at least twenty times, I finally was able to get Debra to say yes and marry me. Debra and I married August 15, 1987, at the Botanical Gardens in downtown Fort Worth in a double ceremony with Debra's sister Brenda and her husband, James. The four of us, along with Whey and Johnny, had been sharing a place.

I had called Dad with the date about six months before the wedding and told him I knew he was busy and would understand if he could not make it. He called back after checking his schedule and said, "You're not going to believe this, but I play Billy Bob's that night."

Billy Bob's, which billed itself as "the World's Largest Honky Tonk," just so happened to be in the Stockyards Historic District on the north side of Fort Worth. So Dad, Jessi, and Shooter were able to be there, along with my mom and her husband.

Whey was junior groomsman, and Johnny was ring bearer. Debra's niece, Jennifer, and nephew, Hunter, walked with Whey and Johnny and also were part of the wedding. My brother Buddy dug up a sound system the day before so Jessi could sing a couple of songs during the ceremony. Bud had set up the electric piano perfectly, but nobody noticed before the ceremony that Whey, who was six, decided he wanted to play the piano. He tried to turn on the piano but couldn't despite all the buttons he had pushed.

When Jessi started playing during the ceremony, there was

a big echo. But Jessi played it cool like a pro throughout. It turned out that Whey's efforts were recorded on the wedding video. When Bud saw the video later, he called me and said, "See, I told you it wasn't my fault. It was your son's. You need to call Jessi right now and tell her."

The night of the wedding, both wedding parties and family went to Billy Bob's for Dad's show, and he announced on stage that it was our wedding night and everyone applauded for us. During the show, we were sitting at a table with Debra's maid of honor, Cassandra, who was a strikingly beautiful, redheaded actress and a real tease. She wiggled around next to me until she pulled her bra out from under her top, and then she handed the bra to me and told me to ask Debra to put it in her purse. My uncle James D. and his wife Helen were sitting behind me, and I turned around in time to see James D.'s mouth wide open and Helen clocking him on the side of his face.

After the show, we said our good-byes to Dad, Jessi, and the family—while Cassandra teased with the band—and went our separate ways.

19

BYPASS TO BUST

Dad gave us a scare in October 1987. He was playing two shows at the Crazy Horse Steak House in Santa Ana, California. He typically didn't do two shows, but the Crazy Horse was a small venue and the owner, Fred Reiser, would charge high dollar for a meal and a show so he could pay Dad to play there.

Between shows, Dad was feeling weak and started having chest pains. A doctor was called in, and he told Dad that he might be having a heart attack and needed to get to a hospital. Buddy was with Dad on that trip, and he started crying. I would have been crying, too, if I would have witnessed that happening to our dad.

Doctors put a stent in one of his coronary arteries and instructed him to give up smoking. Debra and I went to Nashville to visit Dad and Jessi, and he told Jessi to get the ashtrays out for us. I told her that wasn't necessary.

"No, you can smoke," Dad told me.

"No," I said. "We don't smoke in the house. We'll go outside."

Jessi had been waiting all those years for a smoke-free house, and it wouldn't hurt us to smoke on the back porch. Dad, I could tell, wanted us to smoke inside and fill the room with smoke so he could get a few whiffs. When Debra and I went outside with our cigarettes, he closely trailed us so he could breathe in some of our smoke.

He took us and other family members out to a restaurant. Every once in a while, Dad would go outside and walk around. I suspected he was sneaking a smoke.

Dad tried to convince me to quit smoking, too, and shared his method of quitting. He said the urge for a cigarette lasted for seven minutes. Each morning, he would take half of a five-milligram Valium to lessen the urges during the day. I gave up cigarettes for a year and a half until a significant life event happened that caused me to feel the need to either pick up a cigarette or a gun.

Debra and I made another trip to Dad and Jessi's for Thanksgiving in 1988. No sooner had we gotten back to Texas and walked through the front door with our luggage than Jennifer called.

"Terry, uh...Terry, uh...Terry..."

"Just spit it out," I told Jennifer. "What's going on?"

"Dad's in the hospital," she said. "They're doing open-heart surgery in the morning."

"We're headed back," I said.

It was an eleven-hour trip to Baptist Hospital, which was where my son Johnny had been born. By the time we arrived,

Dad had undergone triple-bypass surgery and was recovering in the Intensive Care Unit. Jessi was on the opposite side of the bed, next to Dad's head. I stood at the foot of the bed and got lost momentarily in all the wires and beeping lights.

"It's weird, isn't it?" Dad asked.

I agreed with him.

"You want to see something funny?" he asked.

I answered, "What could be funny about this?"

"Jessi," Dad said looking to his side, "touch my thing."

"Waylon!" she said.

"Touch my thing," Dad told her again.

She did, over the top of the sheet. The beeping from the heart monitor increased dramatically. When Jessi pulled her hand back, the beeping returned to normal.

"Wasn't that funny?" Dad asked with a third grader's grin.

I had to admit it was funny.

Dad said he was feeling fine and that his feet were warm for the first time in years. Ever since I had moved to Nashville as a teenager to live with Dad, he had complained about his feet being cold, whether it was at home or on the bus. Dad would take off his boots and put on an extra pair of socks, and sometimes two. We thought it was a temperature problem. When you're as coked up as he was, you tend to get hot and sweat more. His upper body was fine, but his feet were constantly cold. The surgery revealed that he actually had a problem with his blood circulation.

Debra and I stepped out into the hallway with Jessi, and she told us that Cash had stopped by to visit before the surgery. Dad had described to Cash how he had been feeling, and

Cash told the doctors that he had been experiencing some of the same symptoms as my dad. The doctors gave him a good looking over and determined that he needed triple-bypass surgery right away too. Cash was on the far end of the same hallway.

At first, I freaked out and got pissed off. I asked, not in a hushed tone, "What are they trying to do—get their monthly quota? Did he really need surgery?"

A doctor came and went over Dad's condition and assured me that surgery absolutely was necessary.

"Why don't you go visit Cash?" Jessi suggested.

Debra and I went to see John. June was in the room with him.

"How you doing?" I asked John.

"I'm doing fine," he said.

Medical tape was all over one of his thumbs.

"What'd you do to your thumb?"

"I got a blister from pushing this button that feeds me morphine," he answered. "So I just taped the sucker down."

I looked, and there was medical tape holding the button down.

We left a couple of days later with Dad still in ICU but doing well. He and Cash were supporting each other.

After Dad left the hospital, James Garner stayed in contact with him. Dad had known Garner for years. They had made a TV special together that Bud and Julie were in. They also had performed a live show at Mr. Lucky's, with Garner singing a duet with Dad.

Garner had undergone bypass surgery, and he was the guy Dad would call when he had questions during his recovery. If

Dad felt something was weird, James would tell him whether it was normal or if he needed to have a doctor check him out.

Dad called us in Texas and asked how many trips around the tennis court at Southern Comfort would be needed to walk a mile. He was supposed to exercise in the swimming pool and walk one mile each day, and he wanted to make sure he walked exactly one mile. Nothing less, and definitely nothing more.

Looking Out for Moon

Dad fired Moon around 1988. They were in Vegas, and Dad was in a casino when Moon walked up to him all drunk. Dad fired him right in the middle of the casino. They cussed each other and parted ways, but Dad kept Moon on salary.

Marty Stuart hired Moon to go on the road with him, and when Dad got wind Moon had been hired, he called Marty and told him that he had fired Moon to save Moon from himself.

"It's best he is at home," Dad told Marty. "He can be in on recording sessions and if he wants to show up at a special event, okay. But as far as hiring him to go out on the road, nobody's going to do that but me. Moon's taken care of. Send his butt back home."

Mr. Moon passed away in 2011, and I was able to visit him about a year earlier with Debra and Josh.

"I was really pissed at your dad for a while," Moon told me. Moon had kept a large cardboard cutout of my dad in his house, and after Dad fired him, he took it out to his garage and stood it facing the wall where he wouldn't have to see Dad. He and my dad made amends before Dad passed away, and after Dad's death, Moon retrieved that cutout from the garage and placed it in his man cave along with his most treasured possessions.

While we were visiting at Moon's, I stepped out onto his porch for a smoke.

"Can you give me one of those cigarettes?" he asked.

"Moon," I told him, "I would do anything for you but that. Mrs. Moon would kill me."

I took two or three puffs from my cigarette and softly set it down in an ashtray. After that, what happened to the rest of that cigarette was out of my hands.

At the end of the visit, as we were sharing our good-bye hugs, Moon said, "We did have a little bit of fun, didn't we?"

"Yeah, Moon," I said. "We had a lot of fun."

The following year, about a month before he died, I called Moon.

I'd heard people say that it wouldn't be good to call Moon because of his physical condition, but I'd known him longer than just about anyone.

"I just turned fifty-four," I told him. "Does that make me an old fart yet?"

"I've got some friends here, let me check," he said.

Moon moved the phone away from his mouth and told his friends, "I've got Waylon's son on the phone here and he just turned fifty-four and wants to know if that makes him an old fart yet."

I could hear his friends telling him, "No, that doesn't kick in until fifty-five."

"No, that don't kick in until you're fifty-five," he told me. "But we're going to call you an old fart anyway."

Mrs. Moon called me back later and told me that my phone call had made Moon's day.

On My Own in Music City

Dad took part in Hank Jr.'s Double Eagles tour in 1989. Hank had stepped into a pile of controversy when he mooned the crowd during a show. The next time Dad was with Hank, Dad walked out for their duet wearing camo jeans, a camo shirt, and a camo hat. Hank asked why Dad was dressed that way.

"When they start shooting," he told Hank, "I don't want them to see me."

Dad's tour with Hank was scheduled to end in October with a pay-per-view event from Southern Illinois University. Dad was supposed to perform a complete set of about an hour and forty-five minutes, but the pay-per-view folks cut his time to an hour. Dad got mad and left. For the first hour of the pay-per-view, there was nothing on screen but a shot of the stage without Dad.

While Dad was trying not to get caught up in the controversy around Hank Jr., Debra and I moved back to Nashville, renting a fourplex to share with Buddy, who was filling a "whatever needs to be done" role on the road with Dad.

"What are you going to do?" Dad asked me.

"Anything but get on a bus and leave," I answered.

I had no interest in going out on the road with Dad. The last time I'd left, I honestly wasn't needed anymore. Things were set up well and everyone knew their jobs and how to do them. I had no desire to work in Dad's office. I don't think his office staff wanted me there, either. Before, some of Dad's employees had complained that I was mistreating them. When they told Dad that I had been yelling at them and demanding too much of them, Dad was sitting at one end of the conference table and I was at the opposite end.

"Is this true?" Dad had asked, looking down the table at me.

"Yes, it is," I admitted.

"Why are you doing it?" he asked.

"I suggest they do something," I explained, "and when it doesn't get done, I ask that it get done. When it still doesn't get done, I demand it get done. Then if it still isn't done, I yell and cuss and make sure it gets done."

Dad told the staff, "Make sure what is asked to be done gets done so Terry doesn't yell and scream."

Perhaps I got some of that yelling from Dad. He had a hair trigger and could throw a good fit when he chose to. When Dad said jump, his employees did, both out of fear of being fired and respect for him. Dad was well liked among his staff. When he'd yell at one of them, they would just dismiss it as Waylon being Waylon.

Jessi also served as an outstanding buffer. She'd butt in at the appropriate time and say, "Oh, Waylon, you don't really mean that."

Dad didn't internalize his emotions. When he needed to blow

steam, he would. And then he'd move on like nothing ever happened. To my knowledge, none of his employees ever threatened to quit over my dad yelling at them. Not so with me, and when we returned to Nashville, there was too much friction between the staff and me for me to think about working in Dad's office.

I did, however, want to make a career in the music industry. I had always been interested in the business side of Dad's doings, and I started attending Belmont University—I'd earned my GED in 1986—and taking business classes. For someone who had dropped out after ninth grade, I'm happy to report that I had scored well enough on the SAT to gain acceptance into Belmont and then maintained an A average.

I worked as a booking agent for a while, booking engagements for musical acts. Then I worked in the telemarketing industry until I landed another job as a booking agent. The latter was going well until the company stopped paying its employees. That tends to damage morale among the workers.

From there, I created Vance Music, a management and publishing company. I chose to use my middle name because I wasn't trying to ride Dad's coattails, even though practically everyone in Nashville knew who I was.

This was the time when "hat acts" were all the rage in country music, with up-and-coming male singers wearing cowboy hats. The problem was, most were gone about a year after they arrived. I wanted nothing of the hat acts.

One such cowboy-hat-wearing singer in his early twenties was after me for a couple of years to manage him. He was having a hard time getting a label deal, and finally I told him that he was just another white boy in a cowboy hat and

I couldn't help him. In 1990, Tim McGraw landed his first record deal, and he has been one of the most successful acts out of Nashville since.

I wanted to find someone with a different look and to that end—though I never could have predicted it—my first act would be a Native American. About a year later, I took on the band the Georgia Heartbeat with an African-American singer named Danny Dawson.

My sister Julie had a club called the Hideaway in Yulee, Florida, off Interstate 95 just south of the Georgia border. She told me she had "found someone" in a five-man band. I drove down to Florida, and Julie was correct. Danny was good. Very good. He could play the guitar and write. He possessed the ability to take other artists' songs that sounded like trash, create a new melody, and produce a hit in the making.

I took a demo of the Georgia Heartbeat to Thom Schuyler at RCA, and when I could see in his eyes that they had grabbed his attention, I flopped down a picture of the band with two white guys on either side of Danny. I followed that with a photo of just Danny, and Thom nearly fell out of his chair. I suggested we could present the Georgia Heartbeat and then peel Danny off on his own. Thom went down to Julie's to check out the Georgia Heartbeat and Danny. Thom liked what he saw, but the deal fell through.

Dad was hosting a TV show at Opryland called *Waylon Jennings and Friends*. George Jones had to cancel late, and Dad asked if I could get Danny to Nashville in time for taping. That was one of those questions to which you answer yes before figuring out how to make it happen.

Danny appeared on the show with Travis Tritt and Lee Roy Parnell. Dad interviewed Danny, and he presented himself really well. He was a humble, polite young man, and that came through on the show. Dad hadn't realized that Danny could play the guitar. Danny didn't take his, because it was packed too far back into the trailer, so Dad loaned him one of his guitars. For the show, the musicians would rehearse their numbers with the cameras rolling, and then perform them a second time to be aired. Danny really impressed Dad.

"Why didn't you tell me he could play guitar, too?" Dad asked.

I replied, "I've been trying to tell you he's the full package—singer, songwriter, and great guitar player."

Things didn't pan out with Danny, though. In my opinion, the rest of the members of the Georgia Heartbeat grew jealous of the attention Danny was beginning to receive. We had a guy responsible for depositing the money from merch sales, and then I would write checks out to the band members. The merch guy didn't deposit the money like he was supposed to, and checks started bouncing. That caused a big fuss and we parted ways with the band. But we kept Danny, who is still one of the best musicians I know.

Like my sister Julie told me, "When Danny sings one of George Jones's songs, I tell you, he outsings George Jones."

Thom Schuyler offered me a job as a talent scout for RCA in 1995. He wanted me to cover the Eastern corridor of Tennessee, Alabama, Georgia, and Florida. I told Thom I'd do that except I wouldn't be responsible for Nashville. I didn't want to deal with hundreds of wannabe singers coming to town each year and eating up all my time and privacy. That had nothing to do with being Waylon's son; that was just the way it worked in Nashville, and I didn't want that headache.

Thom granted my wish, and I began scouting talent for RCA.

Busted—But in a Better Way

Prior to fall 1989, Jessi commissioned artist Jim Branscum to create a cast bronze bust of Dad to be displayed at Southern Comfort. Branscum also made an awesome pencil drawing of Dad holding his guitar. Out of the one hundred prints made of that drawing, I have number nine.

For the night of the bust unveiling, Jessi arranged to have the event catered by a high-end restaurant. There was a taco bar with fancy tacos, including fourteen types of cheeses. Jessi told me to start eating so the others would follow and get the event rolling.

Johnny Cash was there, wearing a slicker and sitting by the pool. He waved me over to him.

"Can I bum a cigarette?" he asked.

"If I give you one, Dad will kill me," I told him. "You both had those heart surgeries and you both quit smoking. I love you, but I can't do it."

Johnny even tried, unsuccessfully, to convince Debra and Buddy to give him a cigarette.

Cash got up and walked toward the side of the house and disappeared. He snuck away to a local store and bought a pack of cigarettes. A little later on, he motioned me over to him again.

"Why don't you do me a favor?" he said. "Tell your dad to screw himself."

Then Johnny pulled out a pack of cigarettes and a bottle of Percodan.

"Tell your dad," he continued, "that I ain't quit shit."

Dad had asked Jessi how much the party would cost, and she told him the restaurant would charge around $29 per plate. Well, it turned out she was off by one number—a one in front. The cost actually was around $129 per plate. Dad about lost everything in his stomach when Jessi told him.

As for me, those were the most expensive tacos I'd ever eaten. Maybe it was all the different cheeses!

20

GRANDPA WAYLON

Dad and I had another falling out while I was establishing myself in Nashville.

Even though I wasn't out on the road with my dad, I always kept my ear to the ground for him. I got word that one of Dad's employees was embezzling money from him. Dad didn't want to hear it.

"You're not on the road, you don't know what's going on," he told me. "Stay out of it."

He was so mad that we stopped talking to each other.

It turned out I was correct. The guy who handled the sound equipment for Dad also was part owner of a sound company, and he had found a way to convince certain venues that they needed extra sound equipment, and—lucky thing for them—he knew how that could easily be arranged.

About a year later when Dad found out, I reminded him that I'd tried to tell him something was up, but he had said it wasn't my business.

"Well, when it isn't your business," he told me, "remind me that it is your business. It's your responsibility to make me listen to you. Next time, you make me listen!"

"Dad," I said, "do you know how hard that is?"

"I don't care," he answered. "It's your job to make me listen."

While Dad and I weren't talking, Debra got pregnant. She and I had been looking for a church to attend and found one called Christ Church on Old Hickory Boulevard. With all the singers and musicians in Nashville, the church's choir was amazing. That summer, about four months before the due date, Debra's doctor told her she was at risk of a miscarriage. She'd had two previously, so the doctor put her on bed rest. About the only time she left the house was to go to church.

One Sunday morning in August, I looked over my shoulder and saw Jessi and Shooter walking toward us.

"Jessi and Shooter are here," I whispered to Debra, "and they've already seen us."

Jessi sat next to Debra, with Shooter taking a seat next to me. To be completely honest, I spent most of the time drawing pictures with Shooter while the preaching was going on. Shooter was eleven; I had no excuse.

After the service, Jessi invited us to the house. Dad was happy to see us, and we started talking again, as though nothing had ever gone wrong between us. As we discussed Debra's pregnancy, Dad told me I needed to be in the delivery room when she gave birth.

"That's something you don't want to miss," he told me.

On delivery day, I did as Dad suggested and went into the delivery room with Debra. It was a long day for her, with twelve hours of labor. It was a scary day for me, because Debra's blood pressure was dangerously high.

When it came time for the delivery, something tore. The doctor and the nurse had the baby part of the way out when a shoulder became stuck. They had to act quickly or Debra or the baby—or both—would die.

The call went out for an emergency C-section. Before the surgeon arrived, the doctor cut Debra and blood went everywhere. They were on top of Debra pushing the baby out. There was yelling, and I don't recall any of it being mine. But it might have been.

Our baby boy came out silent.

A nurse took our baby off to the side and I whispered to her to ask if everything was okay. Finally, our son cried. He was then taken to Neonatal Intensive Care.

Debra and I were in shock. She told me several times, "When you talk to your dad, don't let him come down here."

When Debra couldn't hear us, the nurse said, "Boy, she sure doesn't like your dad, does she?"

"What do you mean?" I asked.

"She keeps saying she doesn't want your dad to come here," the nurse replied.

"My dad is Waylon Jennings," I said, "and when he shows up things get hectic, and she doesn't need that now."

The nurse gave Debra a small plastic cup containing three Mepergan pills for the pain and said they would help calm her down.

"You take two of these, and don't give the other to him," the nurse told Debra, nodding at me.

I guess the nurse thought I really needed one, too. Debra took her two, handed me the little cup, and I took the third one. The pills did their job for both of us.

We hadn't named our son yet. We liked the name Justin, but considering the potential that the baby would not make it through the pregnancy, Debra understandably hadn't been ready to pick a name.

A nurse asked for the baby's name for the birth certificate.

"Joshua Albert Jennings," I blurted out.

We hadn't discussed the name Joshua.

"I like it," Debra said.

We say that God named Joshua. His name means "Jehovah is salvation," which has come to carry great significance in both of our lives.

Josh was born at 11:58 A.M. At around four o'clock, I called Jessi and told her we had a son and that he was in intensive care. I was crying and told her how they had cut Debra during the delivery.

"They always cut women," Jessi said.

"No," I told her. "They *really* cut her."

I told Jessi that Debra was resting and that it was not a good time to visit. I told her I'd call when they could come.

About an hour later, Debra was handed forms to sign. One was to authorize a spinal tap on Josh. That made her anxious again, and she said she wanted a cigarette. She hadn't smoked throughout the pregnancy. A few important-acting people with suits came into her room and gave her permission to smoke, considering the stressful nature of the situation. I thought they were more concerned about making her happy so they wouldn't get sued.

Debra wanted a smoke. I wanted a drink. I told her I was going to the Gold Rush restaurant and bar.

I ordered Jack Daniel's on the rocks. I hadn't been in that bar for a few years, but the bartender recognized me and asked what I was doing there.

"I just had a baby boy," I told him.

The bartender spread the news and before long I had probably fourteen drinks in front of me. I didn't want to hurt the other patrons' feelings, so I began working my way through their gifts. The bartender answered a phone call and told me my brother Buddy wanted to talk to me.

"Get back up to the hospital room now," he told me. "Dad and Jessi are on their way to the hospital and you need to get there *now*."

Nurses were coming into the room while Dad and Jessi were there visiting with us. One asked for an autograph. Dad got extremely pissed.

"Unless it is necessary for someone to be in here to take care of this girl," he ordered, "stay out of here!"

Dad later asked a nurse for a bed to be brought into the room so I could stay overnight with Debra. The nurse walked over to the couch and pulled it out into a bed.

"Okay, that'll work," my embarrassed dad told her.

When I took Dad down to where they were keeping Josh, I told him, "We'll go in there and when you step in, you have to scrub your hands and put on a cap and gown and gloves."

Dad said, "I think I'll just let Jessi go in."

I yelled at him, "Dammit, Dad! It's not that hard!"

He went in to see his new grandson. Doctors had suspected there was bleeding on Josh's brain, and he had undergone a spinal tap and seemingly every other test known to man. He was swollen and black and blue. He was wired up to monitors from his chest and arms. The nurse told us he had been crying nonstop for hours.

"Josh," my dad said calmly, and he stopped crying.

"Josh knows it's me," Dad said.

He proudly told that story to anyone who would listen as proof that he and Josh had formed a special bond from Day One.

A New Little Hobby

After Dad had quit drugs, he was able to be a true father for the first time with Shooter. Josh's birth brought his first opportunity to be the grandpa he wanted to be.

We had taken Whey (who had just turned six) and Johnny (who was three) to one of Dad's shows at the old Arlington Stadium, where the Texas Rangers used to play baseball, and Dad had Whey come out and sing for the crowd. But Whey and Johnny were living with their mother when Josh was born, and they didn't get to see my dad much at that time. Josh was close by, though, and Josh became Dad's favorite hobby. Dad would tell us he wanted to spend time with Josh, and he'd come pick him up or we'd drop him off at Dad's and Jessi's.

With all that had occurred at Josh's birth, Debra and I initially were protective of him. Dad was, too, and his and Jessi's house was the only place we were comfortable with him being without us. While Josh was still a baby, he spent a night at Dad and Jessi's. When we picked him up the next day, a very serious Dad told us, "I have some bad news for you. You need to sit down."

Naturally, we expected the worst, although I had not a clue what the worst might have been.

"Josh is deaf," Dad said.

"Josh is deaf?" I asked. "What are you talking about?"

"Watch this," Dad told us and walked over to the crib where Josh was lying.

"Josh," Dad said and clapped his hands. Josh didn't react.

"Josh," Dad said again, and again Josh didn't react.

"He can hear you—he's ignoring you," I told Dad.

I walked over to the crib and said, "Hey, Josh. What's going on?"

Josh looked at us and wanted me to pick him up.

"Oh," Dad said. "I guess he can hear."

Dad had spent the entire evening saying Josh's name trying to get him to respond to his voice.

When Josh was around two or three, he started tuning Dad out because he could tell it bugged Dad. It almost became like a game to little Josh and Dad.

Josh would give Dad kisses, but he'd wipe them off because Dad's mustache would be wet from drinking tea.

After Dad released his children's album, called *Cowboys, Sisters, Rascals & Dirt*, Josh was included with his grandpa on a CBS television special called *A Day in the Life of Country Music*. The show was an outside-the-spotlight look at what country musicians did when they weren't touring or recording.

Dad and Jessi had put a playground set for Shooter that looked like a ship on the hill beside the tennis court at their house. The crew and I installed it together, and if it wasn't for my brother, I might have quit midproject. We had to use a jackhammer to put a kid's play set in because of the shale in the ground.

Dad told the TV crew about playing with Josh and how Josh would sing "Dirt" with him. The crew wanted to film Dad and Josh singing together, but Josh wouldn't sing for the cameras. Dad would start the song and encourage Josh to join in, and Josh wouldn't. After that happened a few times, Dad told Josh, "You're still a better duet partner than Willie."

Dad had made a mistake. He had just given Josh a new bucket and shovels, and Josh was more interested in playing with his toys than singing for America. We had to get Josh to sing part of the song off to the side, and CBS looped it in to what they had filmed with Dad.

At the end of the video, Josh picked up a handful of dirt and threw it at the Martin guitar that Chet Atkins had given my dad. Dad had to pick up his prized guitar and shake the dirt out of it.

"Josh is the only one who's allowed to do that," Dad said.

After filming was complete, we loaded Josh into his car seat and left. He sang "Dirt" all the way home. I enjoyed the heck out of seeing Dad have so much fun with Josh. Dad was happy, Josh was happy, and I like to see people happy. Dad would always say, "I love when Josh comes in the room; it's like the floor raises two feet off the ground."

Trip of a Lifetime

Dad and Jessi's twenty-fifth wedding anniversary took place in October 1994. Dad told me he wanted to plan a secret celebration that would include him and Jessi renewing their vows. Dad wanted all seven of his kids and all his grandkids to gather around Christmastime at Big Cedar Lodge near Branson, Missouri. All seven of us had never been together with Dad and Jessi. Deana and Tomi Lynne had met each other only once before.

Dad told Jessi the part about getting the family together, but not about renewing the vows. Jessi went about making plans, Maureen helped Dad with the surprise part, and I communicated Dad's wishes to my siblings.

Jessi came up with her own surprise idea: She wanted the seven kids to record Dad's "Don't You Think This Outlaw Bit's Done Got Out of Hand" at Barny and Carter Robertson's studio as a gift for Dad. Not all of us are singers, so it took some convincing in a couple of cases, but we managed to get everybody to take part.

We met at Southern Comfort the week before Christmas to take Dad's bus to Missouri. There were eighteen of us, packed together like a bunch of BBs. Whey, Johnny, and Deana's son, Ricki, were the only ones who couldn't make the trip. Whey and Johnny were spending Christmas with their mother in Texas. We managed to load our hanging dress-up attire for the wedding without Jessi seeing us. Jessi gave everyone on board a high-quality Aztec Indian sweatshirt bearing Dad's Flying W logo.

Jessi handed me the "Outlaw Bit" recording, and after we'd been on the road for a while, I told Dad I had a new demo I wanted to play for him. He looked at me like I was weird, like, *Why are you bringing business into this family trip?*

"No, I think you'll like it," I told him.

A few notes in and after Dad had recognized his tracks, he gave me another weird look. The opening lines were mine, and they weren't all that great. Dad didn't know who was singing, and he looked at me as though I'd lost my mind. I'd seen that look from him a few times before.

It took a few siblings' parts before Dad realized what was happening.

"Who's this?" he'd ask, excited. "And who's that?"

We couldn't play that recording enough times to satisfy Dad.

Along the route west, Tomi Lynne started choking on a piece of sucker she'd bitten off. Julie jumped up and performed the Heimlich maneuver on her.

"I never thought I would see Julie being the one saving Tomi Lynne's life," Dad said with a laugh. "Julie, I do think you got in a few extra heaves there after Tomi Lynne had motioned that she was all right."

"I just wanted to make sure," Julie said.

We arrived the next day at Big Cedar Lodge, which was owned by Dad and Jessi's good friend, Johnny Morris, who also founded Bass Pro Shops. Dad had solicited Johnny's help in making the trip extra special.

Waiting for us on a table in each of our rooms was a beautiful, framed photo of Dad and Jessi that had been taken by photographer Billy Mitchell.

Dad was nervous that first day at the lodge because he had yet to ask Jessi about renewing their vows. The next morning, we all met for breakfast and Dad announced that Jessi had said yes. That was big for Dad, because he wanted to do the vows in what he considered the right way before God and his kids now that he was sober.

Dad flew in the Baptist minister Will Campbell to perform the ceremony, Connie Smith to sing, and Billy Mitchell to photograph the ceremony and our trip. Jessi was surprised to be handed a gorgeous designer wedding gown that had also been flown in. Dad asked Bud, Shooter, and me to stand with him as his groomsmen. That was an honor.

The ceremony that afternoon was perfect and incredibly touching. At the reception deserving of royalty, the seven of us kids presented Dad and Jessi with two crystal lead doves on a heavy crystal base on which was engraved,

> Through the joy and the tears you flew together
>   through the years
> Happy 25th Anniversary
> From your children and your children's children
> May we all fly as one

Tears flowed down Jessi's face, as well as most of ours.

We shared a beautiful dinner, with Johnny Morris and his wife, Jeanie, joining us. There was a head table, with Dad,

Jessi, Johnny, Jeanie, Reverend Campbell, Connie, and Dad and Jessi's road manager, David Trask. The kids and grandkids sat in front at a long table joined to the head table. We had a near incident when a conversation went into territory that Julie didn't appreciate. She wanted to go across the table at someone who had married into the family, but she was sitting between Debra and me, and we each grabbed her and took her outside to cool off. Dad came to me later and asked what had happened, and I told him. He got a big laugh and thanked Debra and me for getting Julie outside.

All in all, Dad's surprise couldn't have come off any better, and he was very pleased with how the ceremony turned out.

We spent the next day on a trail ride that Jessi had arranged and antique shopping. That night, we were told to wake up early the next morning for a special treat.

Johnny arranged for us to visit Dogwood Canyon, a stunning nature park in the Ozarks. After driving through the front entrance, we were greeted by families of eagles. We all got onto a flatbed trailer, and a tractor pulled us down a long dirt road. Eagles soared above us as we enjoyed the scenery en route to a stream below a bridge and waterfalls. A camp had been set up like an old chuck wagon, and Johnny's staff members helped us barbecue and fish for rainbow trout. It was a honey hole of Johnny's, and as soon as our lines hit the water, we'd have trout ready to be reeled in.

Josh caught his first fish, and we sent it off to be mounted. Julie caught a fish, too. She let us all know by yelling and running in the opposite direction of the fish. Julie didn't know how to reel in the fish, so she instead took off running to bring the fish to land. Unfortunately, as Julie ran for probably fifty yards, the line kept releasing, so she didn't gain any ground on the fish. Debra chased her down and helped her land her catch.

We headed back to Southern Comfort the next morning to spend Christmas together. We enjoyed the trip and spending the holidays together. We'd never done anything like that, and it was a time that I look back on and appreciate, because we didn't know we wouldn't have that opportunity again.

21

THE FINAL TOUR

Debra and I had been discussing the idea of opening a restaurant in Nashville. When we thought we had a good plan in place, we pitched it to Dad and he was all for it. I'm an inclusive sort, and I wanted there to be a job at the restaurant for each of Dad's children so it would be a complete family business.

The restaurant would be like a Hard Rock Café before Hard Rock came to Nashville.

Patrons would enter underneath Dad's Flying W logo. The restaurant would be to the right, and to the left would be a museum. Dad kept mementos in a second-floor museum above a wax museum at the end of Music Row, but we wanted to display his keepsakes along with some of Cash's at the restaurant.

A lot of tourists were coming to Nashville at that time, and we picked out a site near Opryland and down the street from the Nashville Palace. There was a building there with a small amusement park. We were going to wipe out the building and park and construct our own building with parking places down one side for Dad's buses.

We put together a proposal to present to investors. Bob Sikora, the owner of Magoo's in Arizona, told us how much silverware and dishes and the like we would need. Bob helped us come up with a budget of $1 million.

We had everything ready to present to an entrepreneur named Jim Abercrombie, whom we hoped would be the main investor. We met at Dad's office and then went to Dad and Jessi's for dinner. Jessi invited her sister Sharon to be there, too. Dad was real good with people in business dealings, and our meeting and dinner went well. Mr. Abercrombie told us he would let us know his decision the next day.

I called his hotel the next day, and he wasn't there. I did some calling around and learned that he had gone off to Florida with Sharon to instead invest in her art gallery project.

We had another investor from Texas in line, but the cost and overhead were too much for his taste, and the restaurant never happened. That turned out to be a blessing. Within a couple of years, the Cumberland River flooded our proposed site, and we would have lost almost everything in the museum. Also, when Nashville renovated its downtown in the '90s, the businesses out around Opryland began losing money.

Dad endorsed another restaurant that never opened. The woman behind the project signed a one-year lease. After a year of remodeling the building, her lease wasn't renewed.

Marylou Hyatt resigned her job as Dad's office manager in the midnineties after they got into an argument and both decided the time had come for her to leave. Marylou had worked for my dad for two decades, and her departure impacted virtually every part of his life. She was at the core of everything that had to do with Dad's very complicated life—overseeing his career, his office, his employees, his business ventures, Southern Comfort, and Waylon Jennings Enterprises. If it had to do with Dad, it went through Marylou. She had worked for Dad since the midseventies, and she knew everything about him professionally and personally. He completely trusted her. Record executives knew that speaking to Marylou was the same as speaking to Waylon; if something came from Marylou, it might as well have come from Waylon.

Dad, as well as everyone else around him, did not anticipate the full effects of Marylou resigning. Without Marylou, things weren't getting done, people weren't being communicated to properly, and the business side no longer ran smoothly. It wasn't too long before Dad went to visit Marylou. In typical Dad fashion, he asked her, "Why did you leave me? Nobody leaves me. You need to come back." Marylou reminded Dad that they had mutually agreed she should resign.

"Hell, Marylou," Dad said. "We were just fighting, that's all."

But Marylou would not come back to work for Dad. He tried several different ways to fill her shoes, but there wasn't anyone who could have all the insight and direct knowledge of my dad that she had accumulated through the years. Looking back, Marylou's job as chief executive officer of Waylon Jennings Enterprises had to be the most difficult job of anyone who worked for Dad.

Business Partners

Although the restaurant idea did not pan out, I did wind up getting involved with one business deal with my dad.

Dad and I were talking about how Garth Brooks handled all his business operations in-house. We recalled how at one point in the early '70s, Dad's Utopia Productions was handling bookings for Dad, Neil Reshen was his manager, and Dad's office took care of all the publishing ventures.

"Y'all had it so close," I told Dad. "The only problem was, you were the only act, and it wasn't sustainable. But if we would have been booking and managing other acts, it would have been sustainable."

From that conversation, Dad came up with the idea of creating a company called Dreamcatcher Entertainment. Dad put me in charge of management. He brought in Schatzi Hageman, who had a PR company called Hot Schatz Public Relations, to handle the publicity. Dad would be the name that brought artists in. We each were one-third owners, and Dad also was a client.

Our first act was Shawn Jones, a talented singer, songwriter, and guitar player Dad had discovered in California. Dad wanted to put on a showcase for Shawn, but it was a tough time of year; the only person who showed up was RCA rep Sam Ramage, and he passed. We tried to find other acts, but I guess it wasn't meant to be.

Toward the end of our Dreamcatcher run, Dad experienced some health problems. I was living in Franklin, Tennessee, and working in Nashville, and I'd stop by Dad and Jessi's every morning and talk to Dad before heading into town. He would offer me coffee, and I would refuse.

"I don't drink that stuff because it makes me nervous," I'd tell him.

"That's why we drink it," he'd say.

One morning Jessi called me at home and told me, "Get over here right now." I didn't ask why and raced to their place.

Dad didn't know who he was. About all he knew was that he was *not* going to the hospital, no matter how much we tried to convince him to go see a doctor.

So I said, "Hey, Dad, we're going to the office."

Jessi and I had to walk him to the car.

"We're going to the office, right?" he asked.

"Yeah, Dad, we're going to the office."

When I didn't take a turn that would have taken us to the office, he let me know about it.

"It's okay," I said. "I can double back."

When we pulled into the hospital, he realized where we were, but, surprisingly, he seemed cool with it.

They put Dad into a room and asked him, "What day is it?"

He didn't know.

"What year is it?"

He didn't know.

"Who is the president?"

He didn't know that, either.

They eased him into an MRI machine and he started freaking out because he was claustrophobic. They pulled him back out, calmed him down, and were able to complete the MRI.

Afterward, back in his room, he was feeling better. He

knew the day and the year. When the doctor asked who was president, Dad said, "I don't know, but he's an asshole." It was Bill Clinton, and I always let each individual decide for himself whether Dad answered the doctor's question correctly.

The doctor pointed at me and asked Dad if he knew who I was.

"Yes," Dad said. "That's Terry."

"Is that correct?" the doctor asked me.

"Yes," I said, "but he usually calls me Shooter."

Dad laughed.

We never were told for sure what had happened. Dad apparently had a blood clot that broke free. I've wondered if the clot got jarred loose the first time they tried to place Dad in the MRI machine and his claustrophobia kicked in. I've also wondered if Dad suffered ministrokes. He would be sharp and then go into a daze. We would ask him a question and he'd start to answer, kind of zone out, and then circle back around to our question. Those little lapses would make him mad, and he'd get grumpy toward Jessi.

I think he was beginning to see his mortality, and that got to him.

Dad did have a spiritual side to him. I've always considered "I Do Believe," which was on the Highwaymen's album called *The Road Goes On Forever*, to be his religious song. That song came from a question posed to my dad by Will Campbell.

"I Do Believe" starts out, "In my own way, I'm a believer." Dad once said it was the best song he ever wrote.

Dad, Jessi, Shooter, and Connie Smith took a trip to Israel in 1993. He didn't talk about religion with us, but after he came back from that trip, he told Debra and me, "There was something special there, something supernatural." He said he could literally feel it in his soul. I've since realized what Dad was trying so hard to explain to us. He felt the glory of God.

Into Retirement

Dad also underwent carpal tunnel surgery in June 1994, which we later learned he didn't need. That surgery messed up his guitar playing. His feet were swelling, too, and he could have trouble walking. He was diagnosed with diabetes, and he had to take insulin and check his blood sugar frequently.

In late '96, Debra and I didn't feel that financially we could stay in Tennessee. I'd also been undergoing tests of my own, because I had been feeling run-down and weak. So we moved back to Texas. On one of our visits back to Nashville to see Dad and Jessi, Dad and I were sitting on the back porch, and he got to blowing off steam about how artists were selling two million albums and how Garth Brooks was selling out shows left and right.

"Why can't I be doing that?" he asked.

"You're Waylon Jennings, and they're all trying to catch you," I told him. "You trying to catch them is like catching your own tail. They're trying to get to where you already are."

Dad was concerned about his health affecting his ability to tour, too. After his bypass surgery, he had clauses written into his contracts that allowed him to cancel shows with thirty days' notice for health reasons. He would book a month of shows and stress about the schedule. He was having to cancel increasingly more shows, and I don't think he was enjoying the tours anymore. I told Dad he needed to retire, and he immediately disagreed. I said he needed to hear me out.

"Frank Sinatra retired six times," I said. "Retire and remove all the baggage you're carrying."

"If I get rid of my band," he argued, "I won't be able to find another band if I do come out of retirement."

"Everyone in your band will be there if you un-retire," I said. "If I'm wrong, there will be a line down Music Row of musicians who will want to be on that tour with you."

Waylon called for Jessi and asked her tell his office that he was retiring.

"That's great," Jessi said. "I'm going to pray."

Everyone but the office staff and Jigger were laid off.

"What do I do now?" he asked me.

"Duets. Commercials."

"Commercial people don't come to me anymore," he said.

"They don't come to you because you said no so often," I told him. "Did it occur to you that these were friends of yours and they knew if they kept sending you commercial requests, it'd make you mad? If you tell them to bring the offers, they'll bring them to you."

This time, I was correct. Actually, I was correct about both the commercials and retiring.

The commercial offers did begin pouring in again. One was a Pizza Hut commercial he did with Willie for their stuffed-crust pizza. It was a stupid commercial. It was a good thing they were already legends when they made it.

The retirement was good for Dad, too. It allowed him to

spend more time with his family and to take family vacations. He was able to be around Shooter more. With the time off and the scheduling stress eliminated, Dad seemed to be getting healthier. Those were some of the happiest times of his life.

Promise Kept

In January 1998, I was diagnosed with hepatitis C and told I had three years to live.

I followed every doctor's order down to the smallest detail and went through my first interferon treatment. I was one of the few people who had a bad reaction to interferon, and I had to start taking a lot of pain medication.

I began a six-month treatment, saw more specialists than I can remember, and was placed into a study for which only patients who were off the charts qualified because it involved dangerous medicine. Three times a week I received interferon in my leg to make sure a vein wasn't hit. The second treatment consisted of a big shot of interferon weekly and a Ribavirin pill taken twice daily.

During the middle of those treatments, I had a car accident in which I hit a truck that didn't have its lights on. I've never figured out where that truck came from. It was a Dodge Ram that read "Dodge" on the side and "Ram" on the front. I like to say that if the truck would have read "Ram" on the side and "Dodge" on the front, I would have dodged it instead of ramming it.

The wreck put me in the hospital in Cardiac Intensive Care with a bruised heart. Dad called me before I was discharged, and I gave him the good news that I was still alive and being sent home.

My hepatitis battle was so difficult that doctors weren't expecting me to make it to the next month's visit. They would tell Debra and her parents about people in my situation who would be walking toward the refrigerator and just drop over dead. Apparently, most would die in their sleep, and the doctors would tell me that's what could happen in my case, most likely from kidney failure because the kidneys can shut down when they detect something major going wrong in the body.

My in-laws, Kermit and Tony, became our rock. They were involved in every aspect of my treatments, liver biopsies, and doctor visits. They drove us from Austin to Houston each month for my appointments.

One of the side effects of the medications was experiencing paranoia. I would wake up and remain in my bedroom because I thought everyone outside the door was mad at me. Not until Debra or someone else would come into my room to check on me would I realize they weren't mad. The pain was so bad that I'd tell Debra, "If my head would just explode, I'd feel better."

I was taking Dilaudid, OxyContin, Percodan, Percocet, and other drugs. There were so many opiates in my system that doctors put me on Desoxyn to keep me awake. For a period of time, I used an electric wheelchair. One weird thing that we couldn't figure out was that my viral load on test results would go up and up and up, past where I should be dead. When I'd return for my next month's appointments, doctors would tell Debra they were surprised to see me.

I had numerous liver biopsies, and they showed damage and

scarring in my liver. But I never was evaluated for a transplant, because I was considered a terminal case and wouldn't have been given a new liver anyway.

Debra, for one, would not accept that I was going to die. The doctors believed she was in denial, but she kept praying and telling God, "You know I can't accept what the doctors are saying. And I know when I married Terry, You made me a promise that we would grow old together."

Current evidence suggests that God kept that promise.

My treatments lasted three years, and it took a couple of more years to get off the pain pills I was taking. Before I got off the pills, I went to the dentist. I'm not a liar, and when he asked what medications I was taking, I gave him the full list.

"This is enough to kill you," he said, amazed.

The way my doctor explained it to me—and I'm no medical person, so I yielded to his expertise—I was in such enormous pain that the drugs weren't making me high because they were regulating the pain. My medicine would have been too much for anyone who wasn't experiencing my level of chronic severe pain.

The Phone Call

The year I was diagnosed with hepatitis and after Dad retired, he and Jessi moved to Arizona.

Sure enough, Dad decided to make a comeback and brought together what he considered his dream team, which he called the Waymore Blues Band. The band was mostly former Waylors. Moon and Gordon Payne were missing, but the lineup included Jigger on bass, Richie on drums, Robby Turner on steel guitar, Barny Robertson on keyboards, Carter Robertson singing backup, Reggie Young on lead guitar, and Reggie's wife, Jenny, on fiddle (which she could play between her legs).

Dad began touring again in mid-1999 and into 2001. At one show on the tour, Moon was snuck onto the stage where Dad, who was in a wheelchair, couldn't see him. They hadn't seen each other since Dad had fired him, and when it came time for Robby to hit a lick on steel, Moon started playing.

Dad's ears recognized that distinctive style of Moon's.

"Moon? You here?" Dad asked.

"Yeah, you son of a bitch," Moon answered.

Dad was turned to where he could see Moon, and Moon played the rest of the show with Dad. Afterward, they made amends. That was a happy reunion for everyone involved, and an especially big highlight for Dad and Mr. Moon.

With my sickness, I couldn't travel to see Dad. Debra and I had decided we didn't want to tell him how bad I was, because Dad had enough on his plate. We didn't want him worrying about me any.

During the '99 NFL season, Dad asked me to go to a Dallas Cowboys home game with him. He had been invited to sing the National Anthem and sit with Cowboys owner Jerry Jones in the owner's box. I just couldn't do it physically, though. It was hot, and heat would make me pass out. I told Dad I couldn't go without giving him the real reason why.

He didn't understand how I could turn down a Cowboys game with him, because I'd gone every time he'd offered previously. Dad had close connections with the Cowboys. He had recorded a duet with quarterback Troy Aikman for a Cowboys compilation album released in 1996. Owner Jerry Jones and his wife, Gene, had treated us wonderfully when we'd visited. Dad had even taken the liberty to write Jones a letter of support after Jimmy Johnson left as head coach, telling Jones that I was the "ultimate, all-time Cowboy fan" and how when the Cowboys lost, I would blame myself for the loss because I hadn't worn my Cowboys hat a certain way.

Dad did not know how sick I actually was, so when I didn't go to the game with him, I hurt his feelings.

We were living in Austin, and we were able to see Dad when he appeared on *Austin City Limits* in the late '90s. Willie and Billy Joe Shaver were there, too.

Beginning in the fall of 2001, Dad's health began to deteriorate as his diabetes worsened. Neither of us was in good shape there for a while, and we weren't able to talk much. I'd call Dad and a doctor would be at his house, or he'd be asleep or unable to talk. Most of my communication with Dad was through Jessi. Debra or I would call her to check in, and she would call us. When we asked about Dad, Jessi would speak vaguely. She was giving Dad updates about me, and she probably was playing down my condition, too. I think she was trying to keep from overburdening Dad and me.

Debra talked to Maureen occasionally. Maureen was still working for Dad and Jessi, and she told Debra that both Dad and Jessi were losing weight. Dad was having difficulty eating, and Jessi was stressing over Dad. In December, Dad's left foot was amputated because of infection caused by diabetes. I was in real bad shape myself at that time and didn't talk to him after the amputation. I heard after the first of the year that he was recovering well and gaining strength. Everyone we heard from was optimistic that Dad was going to make it through just fine.

Then during lunchtime on Wednesday, February 13, my good friend and songwriter Leonard Lowthian called.

"I just wanted to tell you," he said, "that I'm sorry about your dad."

"What are you talking about?" I asked.

"You don't know, do you?" he said.

I responded, "What do I not know?"

"I'm sorry I called," he said and promptly hung up the phone.

"Something's going on with Dad," I told Debra.

We turned on the TV and there, from the banner scrolling across the bottom of CNN, we learned that my dad had passed away.

I immediately called Dad's office. Standard procedure with anything newsworthy concerning Dad would be that the family would be made aware of the news before it was released to the press. But in this instance, the press somehow found out before we did.

Dad's office confirmed the report.

Just like that, my dad was gone.

Josh was in fifth grade, and we took him out of school and brought him home, where we informed him about his grandpa. That was a tough conversation. Josh thought the world of Dad, and Dad thought the world of him, too. They were so close to each other. They were best buddies.

Josh asked us, "Have you ever felt like someone reached inside of you and pulled your heart out? That's the way I feel right now."

I knew exactly how he felt.

Somehow, the sun did come up the next day. But it sure wasn't as bright as it had been.

We had lost my father, and the world had lost an Outlaw legend, one of the greatest singers, songwriters, and musicians to grace God's green earth. As Kristofferson told me, "Your dad was like Mount Rushmore to me." I think Dad pretty much was to all of us.

Love you, Dad!

Who's Gonna Fill These Shoes?

EPILOGUE

I've had two things to recover from: my illness and losing my dad.

My treatment ended in 2003. Then I had to get off the pills I had become hooked on. Looking back, I'd say I became well and sober again in 2005. I suffered through seven years of hell.

I don't think I could say I've ever recovered from my dad's death. Do any of us ever fully recover from a loved one's passing? I suppose the best description for me is the words I've heard friends and loved ones say after suffering great loss: "I've adjusted to a new normal."

After Dad died, I stopped listening to music. I was in such pain that it was difficult to even imagine being able to have a career one day, but I knew even if our prayers were answered and I did return to working, it wouldn't be in the music industry. Without Dad, I was done with music.

In 2005, I was at a friend's house, and his radio was on. A song caught my attention.

"That's a cool song," I said.

"You've never heard that?" he asked, surprised.

"No," I answered.

The singer was my brother Shooter, and he was singing

"4th of July." It was his debut single, and I didn't even know he had landed a record deal.

That began a period of reflecting on my life and the jobs I'd held, and I realized my heart and soul were in the music business. I knew I belonged in music, and I decided that, to some degree, I would always be involved in the business.

I reopened my company under the name Korban Music Group and brought back some of my awesome songwriters. I've added songwriters just as talented. I've never been timid, but with my dad no longer around, I anticipated difficulty in reestablishing myself with the Nashville executives. To my surprise, everyone I've called—whether I knew them or not—has been more than welcoming to me.

Since Dad's passing, I have lost two siblings—Julie and Deana—Julie's son Taylor, my mom, and Grandma Jennings.

Grandma and I were able to spend precious time together before her death, talking for hours about Dad and reliving the many memories we built together. Those conversations provided much-needed healing for both of us. I lived with Grandma and Grandpa after I was born, I was living with them when Grandpa died, and after my many of years of traveling, I believe that God meant for me to be with Grandma in Littlefield when she passed away.

I am happy to say that my other siblings are doing well, and I am very proud of each of their successes. I have always loved them, and I always will. Nothing can ever change that.

We don't get to see Jessi as much as we would like. As of this writing, it had been a few months since our paths had last crossed at a tribute to my dad. As always, we had a great time together.

She was signing autographs, and I was teasing her about not knowing how to spell her own name. Her fans started giving me a hard time in her defense. "This is my son," she told them, "and he can say anything he wants." Then we walked off together.

Jessi was good to Dad—even when he didn't deserve it—and I'll always love, respect, and appreciate her for that.

I loved my dad very much. He had to make difficult choices at a young age. He made a lot of mistakes in his lifetime. We all do. Dad did everything wrong in some people's eyes, but my dad had a kind heart and never intentionally did anything mean to anyone.

My dad also was willing to take chances, and my experience has taught me that taking chances requires faith. Playing it safe all the time keeps you bound up, and dreams come true when you have the courage to take chances.

Dad had faith in me. When he hired me and took me on the road, some said he shouldn't have done so. I'm grateful for that outlaw streak in him that allowed him to ignore the advice of others when he knew what really was best. Nothing could replace the time I spent with Dad as he shared his career and his life with me.

In Dad's later years, after he cleaned up and became a family man again, we sat around and talked and laughed about the stories we lived out together. Dad never regretted anything he had done. "Ain't it great!" he said to me one day. "We can talk about those days and the police won't come here and arrest us. We're lucky we got sober when we did."

We did some things we shouldn't have, but I have no regrets, either. To do so would be acknowledging that I want to go back and change the path that led me to the life I have today with Debra and my sons, Whey, Johnny, and Joshua. The path has been rough, but we're still walking it, and I wouldn't trade where I am now with anyone in the world.

Besides, many of those things that some say I should regret also make up the memories of my dad and the unique opportunities I have come to appreciate more and more. Most could only dream of having a front-row seat for the making of the historic Outlaw movement. I had a backstage pass to witness the success of Willie, Cash, Kris, Hank Jr., and others. And, of course, my dad—the Outlaw of Outlaws, the man credited as the biggest influence on changing Nashville and country music.

When Dad and I reflected on those days, we counted our blessings. I remain grateful for God's mercy and the many concerned fans He placed along our path who prayed for us. As a result of that reflection, I had to admit that I needed to change and repent. That was the first step in turning my life around.

In John 14:6, Jesus says, "I am the way, the truth, and the life: no man cometh unto the Father but by me" (King James Version). My sickness was a very rough time, and I wouldn't wish those seven years of hell on anyone. But I am thankful for them, because that was what I needed to bring me to my knees and to Jesus. It was not being a fan of Jesus that changed my life, but having a relationship with Him. That was what finally freed me from all those scales that had been clouding me from the truth.

In telling the story of life with my dad, my purpose is to share the greatest story of all, which I have learned is complete truth: Trusting and acknowledging God—bringing Him into every area of your life—is to be wise. I am alive because of Jesus.

As the Ol' Man sang so well, "I do believe."

ACKNOWLEDGMENTS

First and foremost, I want to acknowledge and offer my thanks, appreciation, and love to everyone who was part of Dad's and my life. They were important and critical to coping with the challenges in an often crazy and tumultuous ride on the road, in bars and honky-tonks, and in many other unsavory but often happy places!

I want to thank God for assigning guardian angels that protected me from evil throughout my whole life, even when I let the evil in! I would never have lived this long had it not been for Him, and I would never have been able to write this book! I want to give thanks to our Lord, Jesus Christ, for His suffering at Calvary that cleansed me of my sins and made me strive for righteousness.

A very special thank you to Dr. Billye Brim for being Debra's and my spiritual teacher. I love being a WWP, enjoy your funny hats, and we love you and "Prayer Mountain"!

Everyone mentioned here has been a critical part of our life experience, and I offer my undying love, thanks, and appreciation for your support, loyalty, and love over the years. Also, my gratitude and thanks to those who took the time to endorse my book, which presents a brief glimpse into the times that this confused boy had in giving his best to his ol' man, who happened to be a country music icon and legend. As I have mentioned, I love each and every one of you and I will always cherish your friendship and love, and you no doubt know that this is a "forever thing"!

I want to thank my parents, Waylon Jennings and Maxine Lawrence Jennings, for their mistaken marriage that brought me into this world! To Dad, for giving me his blessing to write this book and for all the hard choices he had to make, for letting me be his confidant in this wild ride through life, for the many life lessons, both good and bad, for teaching me that dreams are fulfilled when you have the courage to take chances! I could never replace the opportunities that he gave me, and the memories that we made and will share forever. Thanks so much for letting me be a part of it all. I also want to thank my grandparents, William Albert Jennings and Lorene Beatrice Jennings, for their unconditional love, prayers, and upbringing—and for always having a welcoming "safe port" for me to come to.

Special thanks to my wife, Debra Jennings, for our three-fold marriage, for your strong faith, and for our son, Joshua! You are my partner and soul mate! Thanks for your unconditional love and prayers. Without God, you, and your family, I most likely would not be alive today. You are my everything, till death do us part and for all eternity! I also give thanks to my first wife, Kathy, for our sons, Whey and Johnny. Thanks to my sons, Whey, Johnny, and Joshua, for your love and support and for the wonderful challenges of life that I enjoy in being your father. I love you and I am blessed to be your dad!

I want to thank my siblings, Julie, Buddy, Tomi Lynne, Jennifer, Deana, and Shooter Jennings, for being the unique individuals that you are. But since I am the oldest, I get to boss you around! I tried to never take sides, but I did try to keep peace and unity among us all, and as your big brother, I think I did so.

I offer special thanks to Jessi for being the closest thing to my real mother, over all of dad's other wives. Thanks, Jessi, for accepting Dad and his children as we were, and for constantly trying to make us better people! I now know and understand just how rough we were on you, and thank you for standing by Dad through the good and bad days, for your continuous prayers that helped Dad defeat his drug habit and accept Jesus Christ as his Lord and Savior so he could make it through Heaven's Gate!

I owe an especially big thanks to my uncles, Tommy, James D., and Bo, for teaching this skinny West Texas kid to be tough enough to take on a world outside of Littlefield, Texas.

I want to offer special thanks to my in-laws, Kermit and Tony Heimann, for inviting me into their family and for treating me as an equal to their own children. Thanks for your constant love and support, and for being there for me and my family on all those long trips driving me to doctor appointments, procedures, and treatments. May God bless you both with many more years! I still have a lot to learn from you both!

To my sister-in-law, Brenda, and her husband, James Madison—our marriage mates for life, and for always being there through thick and thin, and for the enjoyment of fun times that leave memories of days spent with our wonderful nieces and nephews, Will, Matt, Toni, and Jamie. Thanks to my brother-in-law, Jeff Heimann, for always treating me like family, being my brother, and for all that you have shared! You are the smartest person I know. I have lots of fond memories of you, your lovely wife Cherie, as well as your daughter Jennifer, your son Hunter, and their families.

I have a special fondness for Reverend Will D. Campbell, for being our family spiritual advisor and counselor, and for reaching out to me after Dad's passing, for all the phone calls and uplifting letters and for helping me turn that tragic time into one of rejoicing. Thank you for your direct line to God and for all your prayers.

In recognition of my dear friend, Ralph "Mr. Moon" Mooney and Mrs. Moon. Ralph, you were the BEST steel guitar player in the world, but also my close friend and running buddy on the road. Mrs. Moon, you are one of the sweetest ladies that I have ever met! Love you both and thank you for the good times that we have had!

Ken Mansfield, you have played a major role in Dad's life and career and I thank you for introducing him to Barny and Carter Robertson and Sherman Hayes, along with Ralph Mooney, Richie Albright, Gordon Payne, and Rance Wasson—what I consider the greatest band Dad ever had. Kevin, we have had some fun times together! My thanks to Marylou Hyatt for always looking out for Dad, and you, without a doubt, had the hardest job of anyone—which was obvious once you were gone. Everything about Dad was affected, and you were missed! Dad always told me, "Marylou is your friend, Terry, she has your back!" Thanks, Marylou, for "having my back" and for being a true friend!

I also want to thank all the Waylors throughout the years. Special thanks to the following people who I have been honored to know, work with, and share such wonderful memories and friendships: John and June Cash and family for always treating me like family and for all the fun memories and times together; John for being dad's loyal best friend of a lifetime; Kal Roberts for giving me your seat next to that beautiful blonde, my wife, and your great friendship; Ray "Boomer" Baker and Edwin "Deacon" Proudfoot for being our confidants, protectors, security, and trusted dear friends! Also, I cannot overlook Randy Fletcher, William "Mississippi" McShane, Ed Lester, and Ray Rider—we were the "Waylon Machine" and you were the core base to keeping that machine working so well! We kept the studio and shows rolling right along, and our memories and fun times can never be replaced! Only Loopie knows our secrets, and she will never tell! Thanks, Randy "Baja," for being the best road roommate ever, as well as my best friend! And to Randy "Poodie" Locke and Michael Schroeder, my fellow road warriors, for accepting me as an equal at a tender young age, for my nickname Groaner, and for your friendship on the road. To Willie Nelson, his family, and extended family—when we were together, we had the best shows and more fun than "the law would allow"! We sure did Rock 'n Roll. Willie, I value your friendship and thank you for your help and for endorsing my book! Aunt Bobbie, you are such a "guiding light" to us all, and you are Debra's and my favorite piano player! Thank you for being such a sweet lady, dear friend, and for bringing my wife into my life! To Kris Kristofferson for all those classic songs, and for being the fourth member on Mt. Rushmore. Love you and your family, Captain Midnight! They told me you were "the Grinch that stole Christmas" when I first met you as a young kid, but I learned it was not true! Thanks for teaching me that *The Rocky and Bullwinkle Show* was written by the coolest writers on the planet, and thanks, Captain, for the shout-outs you gave me on the radio! What can I say about Bobby Bare, for helping Dad get his record deal with RCA and for being one of the coolest guys I've known! Duane Eddy, we met later in life and I want to thank you for all your kindness! I still have your bar stools and I love them. To Susan Philpot Spears for the many rides, mostly from jail! I forgive you for *Ziggy Stardust and the Spiders from Mars*. Love you always, Maureen Rafferty, for trying so hard to always please and honor Dad. God bless you! Thanks, Ann Pardue, for all your devotion, love, and loyal friendship to Dad, Julie, and me. Leonard Lowthian, you deserve a "staff jacket"—a hundred times over—and you are my most interesting and awesome songwriter ever, and a dear and loyal friend, and I will always be grateful for you and your wonderful wife, Kris. Then there are the Crickets—J. I. Allison, Joe B. Mauldin, and Sonny Curtis—you all made our tour band shows the greatest ever and you each left me with amazing memories, along with your wonderful wives, Joanie, Jane, and Louise! Richie Albright, we all made some mistakes, but the bond and friendship you, Dad, and I have will go on forever! Billy Joe Shaver, one of the greatest songwriters, ever, I give my thanks for continually pursuing Dad to the point that he recorded the album *Honky Tonk Heroes*, which truly started it all off. And to Uncle "Cowboy" Jack Clements for producing one of the greatest recordings ever—*Dreaming My Dreams*! Love you, Uncle Jack, Allison, and Niles! Hazel Smith, for being my friend and such a sweet lady to me throughout my times in Nashville. Dolly Parton—thank you for being such an inspiration to us all, for all the great things that you do, and for your kindness and love. I truly appreciate your time in giving such a beautiful endorsement to my book. You have earned the recognition that is given to you, and you are a credit to the music business! Keith Urban, I don't know anyone who appreciates and respects Dad's talent and legacy more than you! Your kindness, time, and love mean the world to me, and it is evident that you put your whole heart into honoring my father and me with such a wonderful endorsement. I thank you and will always appreciate your thoughtful and sincere comments!

Writing this book would have been an impossible task without the help of so many giving and amazing people who made contributions and gave support. Thanks to James Ferrell for showing me the door while I was trying to climb out through the window, and for introducing me to David. Love you, brother! David Thomas for helping me turn my life story into reality—could not have done it without you! I am very honored and blessed to have such an outstanding writer as a collaborator! I am truly grateful to you, Chip McGregor, for your dedicated support, patience, and help in presenting my book to a publisher recognized as "the best"! James Madison, your guidance and expertise have been essential components for bringing a calming balance when I needed it the most.

I am also thankful for having the opportunity to work with the outstanding team at Hachette Books. Mauro DiPreta, your vision, enthusiasm, and encouragement have been a Godsend and ensured that my book gets published. Paul Whitlatch, your suggestions and help have been of exceptional value, in editing, coordinating, and helping me focus on my work and keeping me on track to reach my ultimate goal of publishing this book!

In closing, I want to reiterate my thanks and appreciation to Hachette Books, David Thomas, Randy Fletcher, Kermit Heimann, Jamie Madison, Kal Roberts, Gloria Roberts, Moana Roberts, Jerry Floyd, Audrey Winters, and C. V. Gouveia for helping me turn the dream of writing this book into a reality!